Cartoon Portraits And Biographical Sketches Of Men Of The Day

Frederick Waddy

Alpha Editions

This Edition Published in 2020

ISBN: 9789354360237

Design and Setting By
Alpha Editions
www.alphaedis.com
Email - info@alphaedis.com

As per information held with us this book is in Public Domain.
This book is a reproduction of an important historical work. Alpha Editions uses the best technology to reproduce historical work in the same manner it was first published to preserve its original nature. Any marks or number seen are left intentionally to preserve its true form.

NOTE.

With one exception, the likeness in profile of Lord Lytton, the Cartoon Portraits of Men of the Day—for the most part those of literary celebrities—comprised in this volume have appeared during the past year as illustrations in 'Once a Week.' Biographical sketches accompanied the cartoons in the pages of the magazine; and in collecting and republishing the portraits in a separate and more permanent form, it has not been thought necessary to make any material alterations in the notices that originally accompanied them.

CONTENTS.

	PAGE
LORD LYTTON	1
C. R. DARWIN, F.R.S.	6
JOHN EVERETT MILLAIS	8
DION BOUCICAULT	10
ROBERT BROWNING	12
G. E. STREET, R.A.	18
'MR. SPEAKER'	20
J. L. TOOLE	22
GUSTAVE DORÉ	26
WILLIAM MORRIS	28
DR. GARRETT ANDERSON	30
WILLIAM HEPWORTH DIXON	34
PROFESSOR OWEN	36
THE RIGHT HON. B. DISRAELI	38
JOHN HOLLINGSHEAD	46
A. C. SWINBURNE	48
J. C. M. BELLEW	50
HENRY IRVING	52
CHARLES READE	54
TOM HOOD	64
BENJAMIN WEBSTER	66
ANTHONY TROLLOPE	68
C. E. MUDIE	72
LIONEL BROUGH	74
WILKIE COLLINS	76
ALFRED TENNYSON	78
NORMAN MACLEOD	86
ANDREW HALLIDAY	88

	PAGE
CANON KINGSLEY	90
GEORGE AUGUSTUS SALA	94
PROFESSOR HUXLEY	96
CHARLES LEVER	98
J. R. PLANCHÉ	102
EDMUND YATES	104
CAPTAIN WARREN, R.E.	106
JOHN RUSKIN	108
W. H. SMITH, M.P.	112
THOMAS CARLYLE	114
J. B. BUCKSTONE	116
FREDERICK LOCKER	118
MARK TWAIN	122
H. M. STANLEY	124
J. A. FROUDE	126
SHIRLEY BROOKS	128
DEAN STANLEY	134
MATTHEW ARNOLD	136
HARRISON AINSWORTH	138
J. B. HOPKINS	140
GEORGE MACDONALD	144
WILLIAM TINSLEY	146

NOVELIST, POET, DRAMATIST, ESSAYIST, AND CABINET MINISTER.

LORD LYTTON.

Lord Lytton, whose writings have been enormously popular under their author's several changes of name, was born in May 1806, the third son of William Earle Bulwer, Esq., of Wood Dalling and Heydon. The distinguished author has been at one time Lytton-Bulwer, at another Bulwer-Lytton. His eldest brother William holds the family lands, granted to his ancestor by the Conqueror. The second brother, Henry, whose death was lately recorded, was created Lord Dalling for his eminent services as a diplomatist. The third, youngest, and most famous of the family, is the subject of this notice—Edward George Earle Lytton Bulwer, Baron Lytton of Knebworth. He married, in 1827, Rosina, daughter of Francis Wheeler, Esq., the surviving issue of which marriage is a son, well known as a writer under the *nom de plume* of Owen Meredith. Lord Lytton's other child, a daughter, died unmarried in 1848.

The great novelist was very young when first he began to write. When he was only fifteen, he sent out 'Ismael, an Oriental Tale,' and a poem on 'Waterloo,' celebrating the heroic deeds of Corporal Shaw the Lifeguardsman:

> Meantime brave Shaw usurps the martial plain,
> And spreads the field with Gallic heaps of slain.

The young poet was sent to Cambridge, where in 1825 he won the Chancellor's medal; and after another volume of verse, gave the world 'Falkland,' his first novel. A large part of this work is made up of letters from one of the characters to another; and the old style of heading, 'From the same to the same,' becomes very tedious, as they talk in vapid platitudes, slightly spiced with Byronic morality. The preface is dated March 7, 1827, and the author says in it, he is 'entering a career with no motive and ambition in common with those of his competitors.' How many of them are alive now to witness the goal he has reached? Not one, probably. He said then, forty-five years ago, that he had 'shaped out an empire for himself, which their praise cannot widen, and which their censure is unable to destroy.'

Bold words for a young man invading the territories of imaginative literature; but we may safely assume that Mr. Bulwer felt his power, though his first production, 'Falkland,' shows very little more talent than went to novel-making in that time of Albums and Books of Beauty, nearly half a century ago.

His next work, however, showed what he was made of to peculiar advantage. He called it 'Mortimer, or the Adventures of a Gentleman.' His publishers did not like that title; but as 'Pelham' the book went down, and the author at once found himself famous.

'Pelham' was published in 1828. After it came 'The Disowned,' a novel of very doubtful merit, that owed its existence to the author's study of metaphysics. 'Out of that study,' he says, 'grew the character of Algernon Mordaunt.' Then came, in quick succession, 'Devereux,' 'Paul Clifford,' 'Eugene Aram,' a drama on that subject, 'Last Days of Pompeii,' 'The Crisis,' 'Rienzi;' his dramas, 'The Duchess of La Vallière,' 'The Lady of Lyons,' 'Richelieu,' and 'Money.' 'Godolphin,' a story of fashionable life, 'The Pilgrims of the Rhine,' and a political work entitled 'England and the English,' all appeared in 1833; and at this time the author of 'Pelham' became editor of the 'New Monthly Magazine,' a post he occupied for a year and a half. From his contributions in that time two volumes of essays, called 'The Student,' were afterwards compiled.

'Ernest Maltravers' appeared in 1837; 'The Sea Captain, or the Birthright,' the original from which the 'Rightful Heir' was reproduced a year or two back, made its appearance in 1839, and was hardly to be called a success; but 'Money,' first produced in 1840, was most successful, and has, with 'Richelieu' and 'The Lady of Lyons,' held the boards ever since. From 1841 to the end of 1843, the world received from his most prolific pen, 'Night and Morning,' 'Zanoni,' and 'The Last of the Barons.' Besides this immense labour as a novelist, Mr. Bulwer had been busily occupied by his parliamentary duties; had made several bold attempts to earn an independent reputation as a poet, by the publication of several poems of considerable merit; and had devoted himself to politics as a pamphleteer, and to social topics as an essayist. It is not to be wondered at that his health broke, happily to be restored to him again after a time. The story of his cure is told in his 'Confessions of a Water Patient' (1845).

In 1846, his first great work in rhyme appeared anonymously. It was a satire called 'The New Timon.'

In writing a couple of years ago about it, a contemporary essayist drew attention to the attack on Tennyson contained in the poem, and to the retort of the Poet Laureate in the columns of 'Punch.'

This reply appeared almost before the present generation of readers were out of their pinafores; and as it furnishes rather a curious example of the amenities of literature—one poet calling the other 'school-miss Alfred,' and being called 'you bandbox' by his angry rival in return—we will quote the lines of both authors. Doubtless the feud has long since been healed, or at all events forgotten, by the parties to it.

In 'The New Timon,' which, though published anonymously, was well known to be the work of the author of 'Pelham,' these lines occur:

> Not mine, not mine—O Muse, forbid!—the boon
> Of borrow'd notes, the mockbird's modish tune,
> The jingling medley of purloin'd conceits,
> Outbabying Wordsworth and outglittering Keats;
> Where all the airs of patchwork pastoral chime,
> To drown the ears in Tennysonian rhyme!
>
> * * * *
>
> Let school-miss Alfred vent her chaste delight
> On 'darling little rooms, so warm and light;'
> Chant 'I'm a-weary' in infectious strain,
> And catch the 'blue fly singing i' the pane;'
> Though praised by critics and adored by Blues,
> Though Peel with pudding plump the puling Muse,
> Though Theban taste the Saxon purse controls,
> And pensions Tennyson while starves a Knowles.

Tennyson had had a pension of 200*l.* a-year granted to him—most people will think justly. He did not sit silent under this attack. What would be the consequence of such an attack on him now, from such a hand, it is impossible to conceive—such things are out of date. This was his reply, and first and last appearance in the columns of 'Punch:'

THE NEW TIMON AND THE POET.

We know him, out of Shakespeare's art,
   And those full curses which he spoke—
The *old* Timon, with his noble heart,
   That strongly loathing, gently broke.

So died the *Old:* here comes the *New*.
   Regard him: a familiar face—
I thought we knew him. What! it's you,—
   The padded man that wears the stays;

Who kill'd the girls and thrill'd the boys
   With dandy pathos when you wrote;
O Lion! you that made a noise,
   And shook a mane *en papillotes!*

And once you tried the Muses too—
   You fail'd, sir; therefore, now you turn!
You fall on those who are to you
   As captain is to subaltern.

But men of long-enduring hopes,
   And careless what the hour may bring,
Can pardon little would-be Popes
   And Brummels, when they try to sting.

An artist, sir, should rest in Art,
   And waive a little of his claim;
To have a great poetic heart
   Is more than all poetic fame.

But you, sir, you are hard to please,
   You never look but half content,
Nor like a gentleman at ease,
   With moral breadth of temperament.

And what with spites, and what with fears,
   You cannot let a body be;
It's always ringing in your ears,
   'They call this man as great as me!'

What profits how to understand
   The merits of a spotless shirt,
A dapper boot, a little hand,
   If half the little soul is dirt?

You talk of tinsel! Why, we see
   Old marks of rouge upon your cheeks!
You prate of nature! *You* are he
   That split his life upon the cliques.

A Timon you! Nay, nay, for shame—
   It looks too arrogant a jest,
The fierce old man, to take *his* name!
   You bandbox, off, and let him rest!'

Time and a change in the mode of expressing literary amenities on the part of famous authors have made these verses quite curious. We introduce them here for this reason, and not with any desire 'to fan afresh the ancient flame' that prompted them. It will only be necessary for us to apologise for their insertion to such of our readers as may recollect their first appearance five-and-twenty years ago, or may have seen them since.

There was an interval of four years in which Bulwer did not appear before the public as a writer of fiction; but finding, as he says, 'bad habits stronger than good intentions,' he dipped his novel-writing quill in ink again, and set to work on two very dissimilar stories—'Lucretia,' and 'The Caxtons.' The former—having for its heroine Lucretia Dalibard, one of his greatest creations—drew down a storm of angry criticism about his head. The two chief personages of the story were poisoners. To this criticism the author replied in a long and able defence of his work, and an explanation of what he held to be the artistic principles and ethical designs of fiction.

'The Caxtons,' one of his most charming stories, followed 'Lucretia,' and was succeeded by 'My Novel.' At intervals of some years after one another, 'What will he do with it?' and 'A Strange Story,' were published. The latter was completed in 1862.

Lord Lytton has been a popular writer for over forty years, and in that time he has produced above a hundred volumes. He has a good claim to the titles of statesman and orator, in addition to those of novelist, poet, dramatist, and essayist. Such versatility of talent is rare indeed; yet, in all these various paths of literature, the veteran peer has outstripped most of those who have entered the lists with him. He might now rest on the laurels his great talents and great industry have fairly won at the hands of fame. Lord Lytton—then Mr. Bulwer—sat in Parliament first, in 1831, for St. Ives; afterwards representing Lincoln and Hertfordshire. He was created a baronet in July 1838; and in July 1866 was raised to the peerage, with the title of Baron Lytton of Knebworth.

C. R. DARWIN, F.R.S.

Charles Robert Darwin, Fellow of the Royal Society, was born at Shrewsbury, February 12, 1809. He is the son of Dr. Robert Waring Darwin, F.R.S. He received his preparatory training at Shrewsbury School (under the care of Dr. Butler) and at Edinburgh, finally proceeding to the University of Cambridge, where he took his B.A. degree in 1831. The great naturalist comes of a distinguished stock. His grandfather on the mother's side was Josiah Wedgwood, the father of the Staffordshire art-pottery manufacture. On the father's side his grandsire was Dr. Erasmus Darwin, author of 'Zoonomia;' and it is somewhat curious that Mr. Darwin's father and both his grandfathers were Fellows of the Royal Society. He married in 1839 his cousin, Miss Wedgwood. His first work of importance to scientific knowledge was undertaken in connection with the surveying voyage of H.M.S. Beagle. The vessel was commanded by Captain Fitzroy, R.N., who offered a berth to any naturalist who would accompany him. Darwin volunteered, and was accepted. The Beagle left the shores of England in December, 1831; and, after an absence of nearly five years, she returned in October, 1836. The cruise was of a very extensive character—South America, Australia, and New Zealand, the Mauritius, and the Pacific Islands being visited in turn. About three years after the return of the Beagle from her voyage round the world, Darwin published his account of what he had seen—his volume being part of Captain Fitzroy's narrative of this voyage, subsequently reproduced under the title of 'Journal of Researches into the Natural History and Geology of the Countries visited during the Voyage of H.M.S. Beagle round the World.' The other principal works of this eminent savant are, 'Zoology of the Voyage of the Beagle;' 'The Structure and Distribution of Coral Reefs,' 1842; 'Geological Observations on Volcanic Islands,' 1845; and 'On South America,' 1846.

Darwin's great book on the 'Origin of Species by means of Natural

NATURAL SELECTION.

Selection' appeared at the end of the year 1859. Besides the English editions of this remarkable theory, the book has been translated into most of the European languages.

'On the Various Contrivances by which Orchids are fertilised'—praised so highly by Canon Kingsley, in his recent book of travel in the West Indies—was published in 1862; and early last year the long-expected 'Descent of Man, and Selection in Relation to Sex,' made its appearance.

The conclusion to which the author came was that, 'at a remote period, man, the wonder and glory of the universe,' and the monkey, had the same parental relatives. This theory is at first a little shocking, and has been attacked as violently as it has been stoutly defended. Whatever there is of truth in this startling new theory of Natural Selection, whether it be almost of equal weight with a revelation or completely false in its assumptions, time may prove. The names of men of eminence, of great learning and great sagacity, can be catalogued both for and against it.

We shall not enter into the abstruse discussion; but it is a simple duty to record here, that for close observation of the various phenomena of natural history, unflagging energy and perseverance in the search after truth, and great intellectual power, no country has produced a more earnest or more able student than the author of the theory of Natural Selection.

The author's latest contribution to science and literature is 'The Expression of the Emotions in Man and Animals,' a work which even those who feel determined to question its scientific accuracy or soundness will own is as fascinating in its style as it is ingenious in argument and various in its research.

JOHN EVERETT MILLAIS.

The English school of painters in oil, at the present day, may boast of some branches of the art in which it is not at all behind the French, Flemings, and Belgians. Nay, more, there is at least one living English painter who is unrivalled. It is true that making likenesses of dogs and pictures of deer are not to be counted as among the giddy walks of high art. Better, however, jump at a ditch and clear it than at a river and splash into the middle.

Now, in talking of British art to a foreigner, the question he asks at the Academy exhibitions of every year is, Where is your high art, where is the grand in your art? Well, it must be confessed that the grand is generally nowhere in English picture galleries, unless it happens to have been imported. Portraits, animals, fruit, and small landscape are as flourishing, and certainly as good, at Burlington House as at Paris or Brussels; but the Englishman must admit, with a sigh, that he has no grand art to show among the canvases that represent the year's labours of the exponents of British art. The majority of our painters go on, year after year, painting the same old hackneyed subjects, the same familiar portraits, the same bits of landscape. They are so generally successful because they are careful never to put themselves into the way of failure. They clear the ditch, and are satisfied. Should they essay the river? Should they try to rise above silk and satin in metallic folds, above pretty bits of landscape and portraits, whose mission of usefulness is to boil the family pot? Should they try to rise above themselves, above the dead-level of domestic prettinesses in their compositions, and strive to be, some of them, worthy successors of Sir Joshua, and Turner, and the few other great men who have kept the British School above contempt?

The foreign artists have answered the same question abroad by setting an example—they have a grand school, and they ask for it here.

But while so few of our painters become great enough to earn a Euro-

NATURE BEFORE ART.

pean fame, how many shine with a lustre above mediocrity! One of the most promising and original young painters of the English school five-and-twenty years ago was the subject of this notice.

John Everett Millais was born at Southampton in 1829. In his ninth year he entered a drawing academy, and at eleven became a student at the Royal Academy. His first exhibited picture was at the Academy in 1846—'Pizarro seizing the Inca of Peru,' an ambitious subject for a young man of eighteen. During his Academy course, Millais had conceived a distaste for their system of instruction; and with his friends—W. Holman Hunt and Dante Gabriel Rossetti—he set off to look in nature for the effects the old masters had embodied in their pictures. The result of this appeal from art to nature was the foundation of the pre-Raphaelite school. Mr. Millais's principal pictures, executed while pre-Raphaelite influences were fresh upon him, were, in 1850, 'Our Saviour,' and 'Ferdinand lured by Ariel;' 1851, 'Mariana in the Moated Grange,' and 'The Woodman's Daughter;' and in 1852, 'The Huguenot,' and 'Ophelia.' At this time Mr. Ruskin came forward, and defended the pre-Raphaelites with all the power of his eloquence and learning; and Millais was the founder of a little school, written up in 'The Times,' and in his works on art by the greatest art-critic of the age. In 1853 Mr. Millais was elected an Associate of the Academy, and became R.A. in December 1863.

There is not now very much left in his works of the pre-Raphaelite fever of twenty years ago; but his pictures are always artistic and original in composition, and highly skilful in execution. Mr. Millais stands at the head of original thinkers among the R.A.s. He went from art to nature, and he has got a rich reward for his pains.

DION BOUCICAULT.

Mr. Dion Boucicault is a native of Dublin, where he was born on December 26th, 1822. He is the youngest son of Samuel Boucicault, a well-known merchant. His elder brothers have earned in Australia both fame and fortune on the colonial press as newspaper proprietors and editors: one, George D. Boucicault, having been for many years editor of the 'Melbourne Daily News;' the other, Arthur Boucicault, is now the editor and proprietor of the 'Northern Argus.' The late George Darley, the dramatic poet and essayist, was the uncle of these men—so literature may be said to be hereditary in their family.

In 1841, at the age of nineteen, Mr. Dion Boucicault produced his first dramatic work, 'London Assurance.' His later works, 'The Colleen Bawn' and 'Arrah-na-Pogue,' have somewhat eclipsed his earlier productions, and the public are inclined to regard him as a writer of melodrama only. But of all the dramatists who are now living and writing, he is the only one who has produced a series of plays of the highest class, amongst which the following five-act comedies and tragic plays may be recorded: 'Old Heads and Young Hearts,' 'The School for Scheming,' 'The Irish Heiress,' 'Woman,' 'Love in a Maze,' 'Louis the Eleventh.' His comedy, 'London Assurance,' was played for one hundred and sixty-five nights in 1872 at one of the West-end theatres.

Amongst the dramas which have flowed unceasingly for the last thirty years from his prolific pen, we remember 'The Willow Copse,' 'The Corsican Brothers,' 'Faust and Margaret,' 'The Vampire,' 'Janet Pride,' 'Used Up,' 'The Octoroon,' 'The Colleen Bawn,' 'The Streets of London,' 'Rip Van Winkle,' 'Formosa,' 'After Dark,' 'Hunted Down,' 'Arrah-na-Pogue,' 'Jezebel,' 'The Long Strike,' 'Flying Scud,' 'Babil and Bijou,' and recently a little piece entitled 'Night and Morning.'

In 1853, Mr. Boucicault married Miss Agnes Robertson, an actress, and

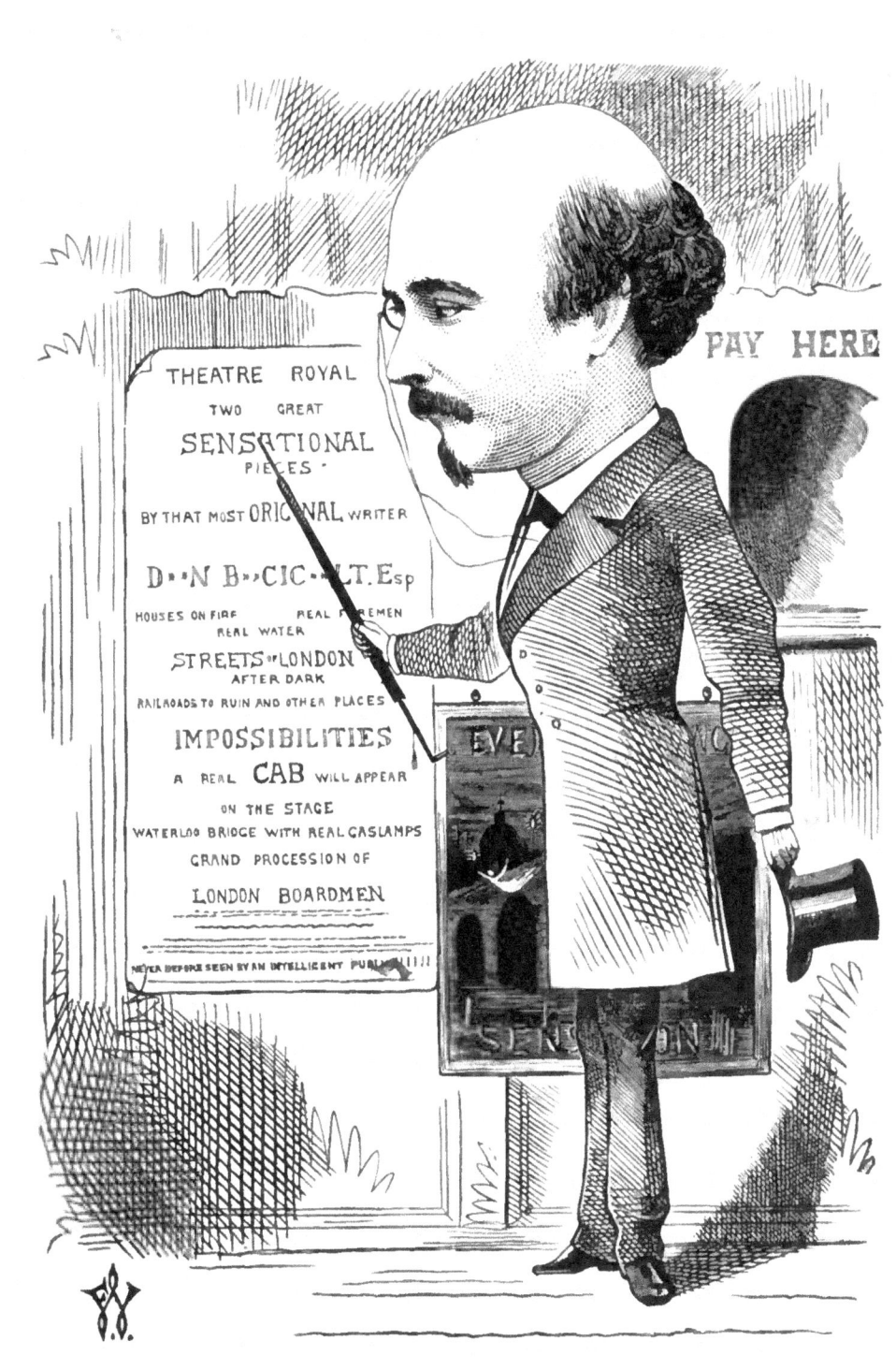

AUTHOR AND ACTOR.

went to the United States, where they resided for seven years. During this period he adopted the stage as a profession; but as his performance of Irish character proved to be his most perfect delineation, he has of late confined himself to that specialty. In 1860 he returned to England, and appeared in September in the memorable 'Colleen Bawn,' as Myles-na-Coppaleen. In 1864 he joined Mr. Vining at the Princess's, and produced 'The Streets of London' and 'Arrah-na-Pogue.' Very few authors have been so uniformly successful, but very few possess the assemblage of powers and qualifications which unite in him to render success almost a certainty. He is not only an experienced dramatist and actor, but his knowledge of all departments of the theatre and their resources is complete. He models and sketches his own scenery, and contrives his mechanical effects. He selects the appropriate music, fashions the action of his piece, drills the supernumeraries and ballet. We shall not forget the effect produced by the crowd of Irish peasantry in 'Arrah-na-Pogue.' He exercises and teaches each performer; and, indeed, instils into all parts of his works a vigour and a life that we rarely find elsewhere. Where capacity and experience are thus found allied with untiring labour, it would be strange if the result were doubtful.

Those who regard a theatrical life as one of idleness and ease may find some difficulty in reconciling their prejudice with such a programme. No life ought to be more methodical.

In 1868, after an engagement in Dublin, Mr. Boucicault declared his intention of retiring from the stage, and devoting himself exclusively to literary pursuits. But his reappearance a few months ago seemed to be the result of a conviction that his 'second thoughts are the best;' the more so that his retirement withdrew from the stage his wife, the most elegant and purest of our soubrettes, whose performances cannot be called delineations: they are personifications of the characters in which she appears, so perfect of their kind, that no actress possibly, in her own line of characters, could be acceptable to the public in her stead.

ROBERT BROWNING.

Strong, rugged, independent; no fashioner of pretty songs modelled upon patterns designed by greater men, no warbler of sweet and soft love ditties, no dealer in unreal and exaggerated passion, no puling complainer of mock sorrow, no dreamy poet of conventional life, is Robert Browning. When, so many years ago, he set himself to make poetry the work of his life, he undertook the task in his own sturdy and independent way. Verse should be his slave, and should express his thoughts as he designed. Now, most poets are the slaves of verse, and can only get their thoughts expressed by a sort of coaxing, and in a roundabout fashion. Then, the life they describe is conventional: Browning's should be real. The motives and springs of action which they describe are simple: those of life are really complex, manifold, various, and overlapping each other. In Browning, we find the psychologist trying to show us in his analysis some of the many influences under which the soul acts. With most poets the soul is, as it were, a river. Browning recognises the fact that it is a mighty ocean. Currents flow backwards and forwards: there are depths and shallows: there are storms on the surface and stillness below, or there are whirlpools below and calm on the surface. The sun shines on it, and the clouds rain upon it: perpetual change is going on, but it remains the same. It has infinite possibilities: it contains infinite treasure. It is ever in unrest, ever flowing and ebbing: ever disturbed, uncertain, and wayward. To describe, to dissect, to observe these currents and moods is the hardest task that poet ever set himself; and it is Browning's self-imposed task. If he has failed, he has failed splendidly. It is a defeat which is a great victory.

All his works, from the earliest, have been in the same direction. The 'Dramatic Lyrics' were the natural predecessors of 'The Ring and the Book,' and 'Hohenstiel Schwangau.' The dramas themselves, so rugged and uncouth, are necessary studies before the later works could be produced.

BROWNING.

'Please, your honours,' said he, 'I'm able,
By means of a secret charm, to draw
All creatures living beneath the sun
That creep or swim or fly or run
After me so as you never saw!'

For Browning is an impersonal poet. Like Homer and Shakespeare, his dramatic power is so great that we lose sight of him altogether. He does not describe; he creates. He does not act before us; but he erects his stage, and presently his puppets perform upon it. His verse is rough and harsh, because he *will* be the master of it. He drags and forces the language to do his bidding. He presses verbs and adjectives to do service which have never before worked for mortal bard. He wants a word, and scorning the customary hack who has worked so long and worked for so many, he looks about to find a better, and having found him, he *makes* him come along and do his work. Thus it is that, even in his best pieces, we are conscious from time to time of a jolt. He is like a driver who drives furiously over rough ground: driving not for pleasure, but because work has to be done. If you want to float lazily on a summer sea, there is Tennyson; if you would glide down the stream without an effort, there is Byron; if you would drive along a smooth road, and admire the hedges on either hand, there is Pope. But if you are not afraid of hard work, rough work, tough work, go with Browning, and follow him while he clears the jungle of thoughts, aims, motives, and passions, and shows you a human heart as poet never showed before.

Browning is not, of course, popular. Popularity he flung to the winds years ago, when he first began to write. We suppose that he must long since have ceased even to desire that really worthless thing—the admiration of the million. True, he aimed at theatrical success; but though his play of 'Strafford' was put on the stage with every possible care, and the principal part taken by Kemble himself, it was a complete failure. His dramas have vigour, clearness of plot, strong accentuation of character, and rapid action. But one feels, on reading one after the other, that they are utterly unsuited for acting. The reason we believe to be their deficiency in tenderness. It is Browning's chief failing. Sympathy he must have, because he sees so deeply; but it is sympathy of a sort all his own. It does not lead him to be tender. It is the sympathy which comes from knowledge, and not that which springs from the feeling of *possible* partnership in misfortune or remorse. It is the pity of a strong man for the weak, mingled with a little contempt. But this is fatal to dramatic success. On the stage, above all we must be human.

The comparatively few who read Browning regard him with an admiration and intensity of affection almost unequalled in modern times. When, twenty years old, Tennyson's 'In Memoriam' burst into popularity, it gained no such enthusiastic admirers as those who hang upon the lips of Browning. When Byron awoke and found himself famous, his fame was like brass beside gold compared with the reputation of Browning among his admirers. These seem few in number, when we count up those who read Tupper; but they are strong in quality. To begin with, it requires a certain amount—we may say, a high amount—of culture before we can appreciate the poet at all; and no small effort of the intellect is needed to follow him through all the mazy windings and involutions of his thought. The story is well known how Douglas Jerrold, recovering from an illness, took up 'Sordello,' and began to read it. Presently he burst into tears, and threw the book away. 'Good God!' he cried, 'I have lost my intellect!'

A profound irritation takes possession of him who begins the study of Browning, against the obscurity of his style. He is obscure, he is involved, he is difficult, he is even at times unintelligible;—and this not wilfully, but because there are times when even he is not able to make language adequate. Words are poor weak things, after all. They are overworked; we expect too much of them. They are too few in number. Doubtless, in a better world, our vocabulary will be more copious, and equal to expressing all our thoughts. And then every man will be a poet. But with the reading of Browning grows one's love for him. *L'appetit vient en mangeant.* And when the taste is once formed, there can be for his admirer but one living poet.

It must be confessed that, in his anxiety to get the full grasp of a subject, he is not only complex, which may be pardoned, but he is also long, which may not be pardoned in any poet. Who, for instance, has read throughout that most extraordinary collection of metaphysical speculations, analytical discussions, and attempts to penetrate and understand the workings of the soul, 'The Ring and the Book'? And why, for the sake of his own reputation, was not Browning persuaded to compress all he had to say into the space of one volume?

We do not want to criticise his poems, or to give any complete list of them. Let us only consider him as he appears to the impatient class of readers—those who refuse to read 'Hohenstiel Schwangau' and 'Sordello,' but are capable of delighting in the shorter pieces.

Has he humour? The 'Pied Piper' of our cartoon is an answer. Everybody knows it. The Piper—

> His queer long coat, from heel to head,
> Was half of yellow and half of red;
> And he himself was tall and thin,
> With sharp blue eyes, each like a pin;
> And light loose hair, yet swarthy skin,
> No tuft on cheek, nor beard on chin—

rids the town of the rats that infest it. As he pipes, they come out of the houses and follow him down the street.

> Great rats, small rats, lean rats, brawny rats,
> Brown rats, black rats, gray rats, tawny rats,
>   Grave old plodders, gay young friskers,
>   Fathers, mothers, uncles, cousins,
>   Cocking tails and pricking whiskers,
>   Families by tens and dozens,
>   Brothers, sisters, husbands, wives,
>   Follow'd the piper for their lives.

He leads them to the river, when all are drowned except one, who describes the effect of the piping:

> At the first shrill notes of the pipe
> I heard a sound as of scraping tripe,
> And putting apples, wondrous ripe,
> Into a cider-press's gripe:
> And a moving away of pickle-tub boards,
> And a leaving ajar of conserve cupboards,
> And a drawing the corks of train-oil flasks,
> And a breaking the hoops of butter casks;
>   And it seem'd as if a voice
> (Sweeter far than by harp or by psaltery
>   Is breathed) call'd out, 'O rats, rejoice!
> The world is grown to one vast dry-saltery!'

Is he pathetic? Read 'Count Gismond,' where his wife recalls that day when he saved her name at the peril of his life, and slew the foul slanderer. She tells it to herself with love-soft heart: one can see her eyes swollen with the tears of happiness, tears that do not drop while she tells it:

> Our eldest boy has got the clear
>   Great brow: though when his brother's black
> Full eye shows scorn, it—   Gismond here?
>   And have you brought my tercel back?
> I just was telling Adela
> How many birds it struck since May.

Is he dramatic? Read the 'Soliloquy in the Spanish Cloister,' when the monk who has nourished a foolish hatred, born of idleness and seclusion, gives vent to his thoughts, watching his enemy at his gardening:

> There's a great text in Galatians,
>   Once you trip on it, entails
> Twenty-nine distinct damnations—
>   One sure if another fails.
> If I trip him just a-dying,
>   Sure of heaven as sure can be,
> Spin him round, and send him flying
>   Off to hell—a Manichee.

Can he stir the heart? Read the 'Good News from Ghent,' and the Cavalier songs. Can he stoop to simple love? Read these lines:

> Nay, but you, who do not love her,
>   Is she not pure gold, my mistress?
> Holds earth aught—speak truth—above her?
>   Aught like this tress—see, and this tress;
> And this fairest tress of all,
>   So fair, see, ere I let it fall?
>
> Because, you spend your lives in praising;
>   To praise, you search the wide world over:
> So why not witness, calmly gazing,
>   If earth holds aught—speak truth—above her?
> Above this tress, and this I touch,
>   But cannot praise—I love so much.

Is he simple? Read 'Pippa Passes.' Is he strong, and rough, and sinewy? Read every line which he has written.

We have, besides the usual throng of verse-writers common to every age, one or two leading poets besides Browning. But there is not one who has a better chance of that best kind of posthumous fame: not one who will so certainly be remembered as the highest product of his time.

G. E. STREET, R.A.

Mr. George Edmund Street, R.A., is, as all the world knows, the architect intrusted by Government with the work of erecting the new Law Courts.

Mr. Street was born in 1824. He was educated at the Collegiate School, Camberwell, and learnt his profession under Mr. Owen Carter, at Winchester, and also under Mr. G. G. Scott.

He has always advocated the employment of Gothic architecture, and has written a good deal in support of his views. 'The Brick and Marble Architecture of North Italy in the Middle Ages,' and 'Some Account of Gothic Architecture in Spain,' are his most considerable works. He was elected an Associate of the Royal Academy in May 1866.

Mr. Street has not had any opportunity of showing his power of dealing with a work of national importance up to the present time. Now, he has the opportunity of erecting one of the grandest buildings of the century.

We are proud of our lawyers, if we feel that there is room for improvement in the system they form part of. They are essentially an English production, and a better article than can be found elsewhere, beyond the limits of these realms.

A long-suffering race, their greatest dignitaries have consented to sit for many generations past in buildings called courts. These courts partake most of the nature of the cucumber-frame and the packing-case. They are hot-houses in summer and ice-houses in winter. They have draughts without ventilation, and windows without light. They are mean, dirty, confined, and comfortless. And they are scattered about in a curious manner, calculated to give as much trouble as possible to the persons who transact business in them.

It having been decided that new Courts of Justice should be erected on a scale commensurate with the importance of the uses for which they were

THE SELECTED ARCHITECT.

intended, there was a competition of the best architects, and their designs were submitted to a committee, composed of more or less competent judges, in the month of January 1867.

The result of the investigation into the merits of the various designs was, that Mr. Street was intrusted with the work.

For a time, what was aptly called the battle of the sites drowned all else; but when the ground on which the buildings were to be erected was once fixed upon, there arose a fresh debate about the merits of Mr. Street's designs, which has been kept up ever since with great zeal and warmth.

This opposition to his designs proceeds, not from the public, but from two or three interested and self-satisfied little cliques, who cannot lose, if they do not gain, by—in vulgar speech—kicking up a row.

Mr. Street has not made an accurate imitation of mediæval detail, but has designed an edifice in a style perfectly free and elastic, and one which lends itself easily to every useful requirement of the present age. He has succeeded in grouping together eighteen law courts and their appendant offices in a design which promises a very fine and altogether suitable building.

Mr. Street's difficult task has been to consult the convenience of both branches of the legal profession, and to produce a building pleasing to the public who will pay for it. The dissatisfaction of professional critics is quite accounted for by the fact that they are dealing with the proposals of the selected architect.

'MR. SPEAKER.'

The first announcement to members on returning to their seats in Parliament last session was that their Speaker had resigned his distinguished post, and thrown upon them the preliminary business of selecting another to assume the place of First Commoner in England, and to be president of their councils.

There have been—excluding the present—only four Speakers of the House of Commons since the death of George III., which occurred above half a century ago. When George IV. succeeded to the throne in 1820, Mr. C. Manners Sutton was Speaker, having been chosen to that high office in 1817, and he remained Speaker down to the dissolution of the first reformed Parliament, in 1834. On the meeting of the next Parliament, on the 19th of February 1835, his re-election was opposed—this first opportunity for a trial of strength between the two political parties being taken. On that occasion, the new Ministry—Sir Robert Peel's—was defeated, the numbers being—for Mr. James Abercromby, 316; and for Mr. C. Manners Sutton, 306. The latter was then created Viscount Canterbury. Mr. Abercromby was Speaker for only a very few years. He retired at the Whitsuntide recess in 1839, and again there was a contest for the vacant chair. The numbers on this occasion were—for Mr. Shaw Lefevre, 317; and for Mr. Goulburn, 299. Mr. Abercromby was then raised to the peerage as Baron Dunfermline. Mr. Shaw Lefevre remained Speaker for nearly eighteen years. At the dissolution of Parliament in March 1857, he retired, and was created Viscount Eversley. On the meeting of the new Parliament, on the 30th of April 1857, Mr. J. Evelyn Denison was unanimously chosen Speaker. Mr. Denison therefore presided over the deliberations of the House of Commons for nearly fifteen years.

Mr. Denison was born in the year 1800, and was educated at Eton and at Christ Church, Oxford, where he graduated in 1823. In the same year,

MR. SPEAKER.

he was returned to Parliament for Newcastle-under-Lyme. On the formation of Canning's Administration, Mr. Denison was appointed one of the Lords of the Admiralty.

At this time the question of Roman-Catholic emancipation agitated the rival political parties of the day, and Mr. Denison was a constant adherent to the claims of the Roman Catholics.

The death of Canning led to a change of the Administration; and Mr. Denison relinquished his post at the Admiralty Board. Preferring an independent political career to the responsibilities of office, he remained in privacy, although several Administrations sought his services.

In 1830 Mr. Denison was returned for Hastings. In 1831, after the lamentable death of Mr. Huskisson, he was invited to stand for Liverpool; and, at the general election of 1831, he was returned for that borough, and also for the county of Nottingham; but he elected to sit for the latter.

During two Parliaments he represented the borough of Malton; and in 1857 he was returned for North Nottinghamshire, for which place he has since continued the member. Mr. Denison took an active part in the conduct of the private business of the House, and, as we have just mentioned, on the retirement of Mr. Shaw Lefevre he was, in 1857, unanimously chosen Speaker; being afterwards unanimously elected in 1859 and in 1866.

Mr. Denison married, in 1827, the third daughter of the Duke of Portland.

The emolument of the Speaker, it may be added, consists of a furnished house in the New Palace at Westminster, and a standing salary of 5000*l.* a year, besides other collateral advantages in the way of valuable pieces of Crown patronage which fall to his disposal from time to time.

Mr. Denison, on retiring from the Speakership, was raised to the peerage, with the title of Viscount Ossington, of Ossington, in the county of Notts.

J. L. TOOLE.

The eminent comedian, Mr. John Laurence Toole, is a native of the city of London, and was born, as he sometimes jokingly says, 'of poor but dishonest parents, you know,' in the year 1831. He is the son of the late celebrated toastmaster, who distinguished himself as much by his 'Silence, gentlemen, if you please,' and by his good and genial qualities, as his son has since done on the boards.

Mr. Toole received his education at the City of London School, and was removed thence at the usual age to become a clerk in a merchant's office. His taste for the drama appears to have developed itself very early in life, for at this time he became a member of the 'City Histrionic Club,' where he soon became very popular. The appearances of the amateur actor were hailed with applause at several metropolitan literary institutions, where he performed in various characters. His successes at Walworth, Aldersgate-street, Hackney, Crosby Hall, and other places, caused Mr. Toole to lay down his pen and put on the buskin as a professional actor.

His first appearance on the stage of a regular theatre was at Ipswich, on the occasion of a benefit, where—under an assumed name—he played the part of Silvester Daggerwood. This assumption was completely successful. On his return to town, Mr. Toole played as an amateur at the Haymarket, for Mr. F. Webster's benefit, taking the character of Simmons in the 'Spitalfields Weaver.' After this performance he gave up his commercial pursuits, and took to the stage for good.

His début as a professional was made at the Queen's Theatre, Dublin, on the 2d of October 1852—now twenty years ago. Since that date Mr. Toole's career has been a series of successes. From Dublin, where he was well received, Mr. Toole went to Edinburgh, and thence to Glasgow.

In London his first engagement was at the St. James's Theatre, then

I HOPE I DON'T INTRUDE.

under the management of Mrs. Seymour. Here he played in 'My Friend the Major,' 'Boots at the Swan,' 'Honours before Titles'—in all of which his rendering of the characters he portrayed was perfectly satisfactory to audiences and critics.

A reëngagement took him to Edinburgh, after which he appeared at the Lyceum, and made a success of the character of Fanfarronade in 'Belphegor.'

After a provincial tour, Mr. Toole commenced an engagement at the Adelphi, and played with the greatest success in 'Ici on Parle Français,' 'Willow Copse,' 'Birthplace of Podgers,' 'Good for Nothing,' 'Bengal Tiger,' and other pieces.

At the Adelphi, great successes were made in the adaptation of 'The Haunted Man' by his performance of Mr. Tetterby, and of a frightened servant in a miserable piece by Mr. Boucicault, called 'The Phantom.' The character saved the piece. After leaving the Adelphi Theatre, Mr. Toole became a member of Mr. W. H. Liston's company at the new Queen's, and contributed largely to the success of that undertaking in the production of several important original dramas, among which perhaps the most notable was that of Mr. Byron's 'Dearer than Life,' in which the actor's representation of Michael Garner again presented him to the public as the legitimate successor of the late Mr. Robson. The popularity of this drama has been very great, and it still continues to be a great attraction, not only through Mr. Toole's provincial engagements, but also when put forward in London, as it still occasionally is. Another successful production was that of the play of 'Not Guilty,' in which Mr. Toole had a prominent character. Nor should we forget a most admirable performance of his in the charming little drama called 'The Poor Nobleman,' which greatly contributed to the success of the piece. Space will not allow of our following Mr. Toole through those many original pieces in which the public have indorsed his qualities as an actor; but we must mention with a special word of praise the performance of Dick Dolland, in 'Uncle Dick's Darling;' and of John Lockwood, in the later drama called 'Wait and Hope,' produced a season or two back at the Gaiety.

Mr. Toole is almost unrivalled in his line at present. In comedy and farce, in humour and pathos, his acting is excellent. He is always amusing, often affecting. There are no parts that show him to greater advantage than such characters as Caleb Plummer in 'Dot,' or Harry Coke in 'Off the Line.' Of this impersonation, Mr. Toole makes one of those perfect pictures of everyday life of the lower class in which he has so often proved himself a consummate artist. But in low comedy and broad farce it would be difficult to find an actor of equal merit. He has identified himself of late with the character of Paul Pry, in Poole's celebrated play of that name. As Paul Pry he keeps his audience in a roar whenever he is on the stage; but he renders the character of the inquisitive gentleman in a quiet and unobtrusive way, quite original in itself. In Mr. Toole's hands, Paul's curiosity is a disease. He does not know of his peculiarity, and his 'I hope I don't intrude,' and 'I just dropped in,' fall not as gag phrases, but as the natural remarks of a man who feels the importance of his business must make his company desirable, or at all events tolerable.

Although, perhaps, the character is not naturally so well suited to Mr. Toole as many others of his well-known parts, he has completely made Paul his own. It is a part in which the actor mellows with time. Mr. Toole has played it many times, and his representation of the prying gossip is now admirable. It is one of the most finished and perfect of his efforts: from the beginning to the end of the piece he seems never to miss a single point.

E

GUSTAVE DORÉ.

Monsieur Paul Gustave Doré was born at Strasburg in the month of January 1832. At an early age he was taken to Paris by his father, and there his education was completed. When quite a boy, he contributed to the 'Journal pour Rire' little comic sketches. Of his pictures, among the first to attract the attention of connoisseurs were 'La Bataille d'Alma,' exhibited in 1855, and 'La Bataille d'Inkermann,' exhibited in 1857.

M. Doré's works are well known in this country, where they have been exhibited both as contributions to exhibitions of pictures by various artists, and also a number of his oil pictures forming a gallery by themselves.

M. Doré has turned his great powers to drawings on the wood; and, as an illustrator of books of imagination by the great authors, is almost unrivalled in popularity. His pictorial interpretations of Rabelais, of Balzac's wild 'Contes Didactiques,' and of that grand work of fiction, 'The Wandering Jew,' are well known and deservedly admired for their originality and realisation of the author's ideal; though the artist's illustrations to the 'Divina Commedia' of Dante, to Cervantes' perennial 'Don Quixote,' to Milton, and to the Holy Bible, are better known in this country.

Though French by birth, M. Doré is almost an Englishman by adoption, and is perfectly conversant with English places and people. He has drawn a history of the metropolis under the title of 'London : a Pilgrimage.'

M. Doré received, on 15th of August 1861, the decoration of the Cross of the Legion of Honour.

Whatever branch of his art his fame in his own country may ultimately rest upon, here the name of Gustave Doré will always be associated—in the minds of those who were among the first to recognise his great talent, and

ILLUSTRATION.

to extend to him their support—with his wonderful powers of illustration. The humorous scenes of Cervantes, the lofty fancy of Milton, the splendid imagery of the prophetic authors of Sacred Writ, have received from Doré something nearly approaching to an interpretation of their authors' ideal.

WILLIAM MORRIS.

We suppose that nobody will deny that the author of 'The Earthly Paradise' has earned the right to be numbered among English poets. Whether his place is above or below Swinburne it is difficult to decide, as opinions differ very much as to the merits of Mr. Swinburne's poems. The style of Mr. Morris's verses is quite as good as that of Mr. Swinburne's, and he has the farther advantage of being pure in tone, while he is classical in theme.

The first work of his to attract attention in a considerable degree was 'The Life and Death of Jason,' a long poem, divided into sixteen books. As its title imports, it is founded on the adventures of the hero Jason, son of Æson, king of Iolchos, whose romantic pursuit of the golden fleece, and love affairs with Medea and Glaucé, have formed the base of so many poetic edifices. 'The Earthly Paradise,' Mr. Morris's chief work, has, although published at intervals and of great length, already become popular. On this work his claim to the fame of a poet must rest; and the very favourable reception the poem has met with will warrant the author in assuming that he is a poet of considerable pretensions to a fellowship with Tennyson and Browning.

We shall not try to review such a voluminous poem as 'The Earthly Paradise' at length; and we shall therefore content ourselves with stating that, to people who have a taste for a poem in four or five volumes, the perusal of 'The Earthly Paradise' will give great pleasure and some profit. The argument of the prologue is, 'Certain gentlemen and mariners of Norway, having considered all that they had heard of the Earthly Paradise, set sail to find it; and after many troubles, and the lapse of many years, came old men to some western land of which they had never before heard. There they died, when they had dwelt there certain years, much honoured of the strange people.'

That such a theme gives a fine opportunity to a discursive poet is patent,

THE EARTHLY PARADISE.

and Mr. Morris has made good use of it. Many subjects are treated in the prologue, and perhaps it is as good as anything in the poem. A general lack of purpose will strike the reader; but for this they were prepared by the author in his introduction, where he says:

> Dreamer of dreams, born out of my due time,
>   Why should I strive to set the crooked straight?
> Let it suffice me that my running rhyme
>   Beats with light ring against the ivory gate,
>   Telling a tale, not too importunate,
> To those who in the sleepy region stay,
> Lull'd by the singer of an empty day.
>
>   *   *   *   *
>
> So with this earthly Paradise it is,
>   If ye will read aright, and pardon me,
> Who strive to build a shadowy isle of bliss
>   Midmost the beating of the steely sea,
>   Where toss'd about all hearts of men must be;
> Whose ravening monsters mighty men shall slay,
> Not the poor singer of an empty day.

DR. GARRETT ANDERSON.

In the middle ages, the work of women was clearly defined and unmistakable. If they were of the lower class, they made the clothes, spun the linen, kept the house; if of the higher, they received the guests, they embroidered, they presided at tournaments, and they were the family doctors. They knew the virtues of those simple herbs which they gathered in the garden and the fields; from these they concocted plasters and poultices for bruises and hurts, which must have been common enough in those days. Nicolette, in the old French novel, handles Aucassin's shoulder till she gets the joint into its proper place again, when she applies a poultice of soothing herbs. For medical purposes — perhaps also for a secret means of warming their hearts when they grew old—they brewed strong waters out of many a flower and fruit. All the winter long—when there was little fighting, and therefore few disorders, save those due to too much or too little feeding—they stayed in the castle and studied the art of healing. With the spring came dances, hawking, garland-making, sitting in the sunshine and under the shade, while the minstrels sang them ditties, and the knights made love, and preparations were made for the next tournament.

Here, it seems, was a fair and equitable distribution of labour. Both man and woman had to work. Why not? Man fought, tilled, traded. Women spun, kept house, and healed. Surgical operations, if any were required, were conducted in the handiest and simplest method possible— with the axe; as when Leopold of Austria had his leg amputated at a single blow, and died from loss of blood.

There came a time when the art of healing passed into men's hands. Then women had one occupation the less. They made up for this at first by becoming scholars. Everybody knows about the scholarship of Lady Jane Grey and Queen Elizabeth. The ladies of the sixteenth century read

M.D.

everything and knew everything. Then, too, under the auspices of Madame de Rambouillet, was born modern society. Learning went out of fashion as social amusements developed. Then women substituted play for work, and made amusement their occupation. The arts of housewifery vanished with that of healing. The occupations of embroidery and spinning disappeared with that of study. In the eighteenth century, woman was either a fine lady or a household servant. If the former, she gambled, dressed, received, and went out; if the latter, she cooked and washed, and tended the children. Of course, the women of the last century accepted, patiently enough, the rôle thrust upon them by circumstances. They were submissive to their lords, were thankful for their kindnesses, and forgave them their many sins. And it was not till early in the present century that the blue stocking appeared, to become a subject of ridicule. This was unfortunate, because the blue stockings, in a desultory, hesitating way, only tried to recover a portion of woman's lost ground. For a long time women who studied were looked upon with disfavour and suspicion. Why could not they make samplers and puddings, and play on the harpsichord? Some of them—poor things!—were obliged to learn in order to become governesses. But, really, what more ridiculous than that a woman should learn the same things as a man? Above all, why seek to change things?

Social prejudices are almost as hard to eradicate as those of religion. It was not till quite lately that the feeling against woman's rights as regards education was successfully combated; and even now there are hundreds of respectable parents who would far rather send their daughters to a fashionable boarding-school at Brighton, where they are sure to learn nothing, than to a place like the Hitchin College, where they will be taught with the same accuracy and thoroughness as Cambridge honour men.

We go up and down like a see-saw. After two hundred years our women are going to become students again; and after three hundred years they are going to become physicians again. Foremost among lady doctors is Mrs. Anderson. In the profession which she has taken up, particularly in those branches to which she is understood to have chiefly devoted her attention—the diseases of women and children—we wish her all the success that her courage and ability deserve. More: we hope that she is the forerunner of many other ladies who will take up the art of healing. Women can become at once nurses and doctors; their gentleness—not greater than that of some men, in spite of what is said—is more uniform: they have more patience; they are ready to devote more time. Only the conditions of things are changed. It is no longer necessary to know the properties of simples; it is necessary also to study the anatomy and framework of the body, to gain experience in the symptoms of disease, to go through a great deal that is repulsive and hard. It is no light thing to become a physician. We do not think that there will ever be a large proportion of women who will have the courage to face the difficulties and brave the labour. Many may, however, learn enough to make themselves invaluable nurses.

So will be restored the mediæval condition. Women will occupy themselves in household work, in study and literature, in looking after and educating children, in social amusements, in dances, music, and love-making. Man—poor, dear, patient animal!—goes on always the same: working for those he loves, striving to keep the nest warm, and caring little enough for aught else.

As for the rest, things are in a transition state, and consequently uncomfortable and disagreeable. Women, finding that their sphere is enlarged, want, naturally enough, to get as much as they can. Nor have they yet learned how to limit their aims to their strength. If they are prepared to give up love and marriage, or to subordinate these—with, of course, the welfare of their children—to other things; if, farther, they are willing to give up those social amenities to which they are accustomed—the concession of small things by men, the deference and respectful bearing of gentlemen towards them—then, by all means, let women go upon platforms, and fight in the arena, side by side with their brothers. Life is a great battle, in which, from time immemorial, women have been spared. If they want to enter it, let them come. But the battle is for existence: they will be struck down ruthlessly; and they will enter it, however well prepared and armed, with whatever ability of brain, *with a feeble and delicate frame.*

Meantime, it is all windbags and nonsense. A few women have got up a cry—partly from a wish to get notoriety, partly from a perfectly intelligible, if unreasonable, revolt against their own position, partly against one or two real grievances. They are the shrieking sisterhood. Their voices alone are heard. Their ranks are not increasing; but they make such a confounded clatter, that we quiet men believe the numbers to be tenfold what they really are.

The way to meet them is to argue as little as possible; to take away as much as possible all power to do mischief (by interfering in subjects in which, rightly or wrongly, they can know little, they have done a good deal of mischief already); to help all women, in every station, to honest work; to secure for women proper pay for work; to concede all that we can. Let us acknowledge at once that women *can* do everything; we may then invite them to illustrate their position. For it remains with them to establish the theory that they can do everything. Meantime, let us remember, and whisper among ourselves, that they have not yet produced—in the first rank, be it remembered—a single musician, painter, poet, metaphysician, scholar, mathematician, chemist, physicist, physician, mechanician, or historian. One great, very great, novelist is a woman—George Sand. Second- and third-rate people of course are common as blackberries.

The best thing that can happen to a woman is to attract the love of a man: the best thing for a man is to love a woman. All the female men in the world cannot alter the laws of nature.

Meanwhile, Mrs. Anderson, who did not shine when she left her own line and went to the School Board, has, we hope, a successful and honourable career before her in her most noble and womanly work.

WILLIAM HEPWORTH DIXON.

The reputation of a very successful literary man might have been made on a fourth of what the ex-editor of the 'Athenæum' has done. In the catalogue of the British Museum—excluding his last work, 'The Switzers'—there are fifty-four titles bearing Mr. Dixon's name. He has, from his first literary effort—a play—to his last book of travel, written successively history, biography, essays, and travel, besides having filled the post of editor of the first among literary papers. His books have been translated into several of the languages of Europe, and there have been many American editions of his popular works.

He is the son of Mr. Abner Dixon, of Holmfirth and Kirk Burton, in the West Riding of Yorkshire, and was born June 30, 1821. Early in life, Mr. Dixon was associated with Douglas Jerrold and the great writers of that day; and, after publishing some papers in the 'Daily News' on the 'Literature of the Lower Orders,' and on 'London Prisons,' he wrote a 'Life of John Howard,' a book that at once attracted the attention it deserved, and passed through three editions in the first year after its publication—this was in 1849.

'Robert Blake, Admiral and General at Sea,' appeared in 1852. Mr. Dixon was also one of the most energetic and able promoters of the Great Exhibition of 1851. His latest works are 'New America,' 'Her Majesty's Tower,' 'Spiritual Wives,' 'Free Russia,' and 'The Switzers.' These works—as their popularity attests—are written in a manner very pleasing to the general reader. The style is lively and discursive—one in which new information on topics of the greatest interest is marshalled with the skill of a practised pen, without the matter ever becoming dry, or the pages tedious to the reader, who, resigning himself to the spell of the writer's power, visits with him the places and people he has described with so much freshness and originality.

HER MAJESTY'S TOWER.

PROFESSOR OWEN.

There is to be seen at about ten o'clock on most mornings, in one or other of the streets leading in a direct line from Waterloo-bridge to the British Museum, an elderly gentleman who walks as if his feet were very tender, and whom most of the persons he meets turn round to stare after. This is Professor Owen on his way to his favourite studies at the Museum, where he is superintendent of the Natural History departments.

Richard Owen, Fellow of the Royal Society, enjoys a European reputation as a comparative anatomist. He was born in Lancaster, in 1804, and educated at the University of Edinburgh. In 1826 he became a member of the Royal College of Surgeons, and nine years later was appointed Hunterian Professor and Conservator of the Museum at the College.

Among other works of importance which Mr. Owen has written may be mentioned 'Odontography' (published 1840); 'Memoir of a Gigantic Extinct Sloth,' 'Lectures on the Comparative Anatomy of the Invertebrate Animals' (1843); 'History of British Fossils, Mammals, and Birds.' 'On the Megatherium,' 'On the Gorilla,' 'On the Dodo,' are among his recent works; besides many other works on various branches of the science of which he is the greatest living exponent. Professor Owen has written many papers for the Transactions of the Royal and various other learned societies. Mr. Owen is a Chevalier of the Prussian Order of Merit, and in 1855 he was decorated by the Emperor Napoleon with the Cross of the Legion of Honour. He is one of the eight foreign members of the French Institute, and, besides, is a Fellow or Associate of every learned and scientific society of distinction at home and abroad.

RIDING HIS HOBBY.

THE RIGHT HON. B. DISRAELI.

It is not our intention in this notice to attempt any review of Mr. Disraeli's political career. As cartoons in this book are chiefly portraitures of men of letters, it is of the literary achievements of the leader of the Conservative party that we propose to speak. The ex-Premier is the author of a number of clever novels, with which most readers doubtless are perfectly familiar. The first of this series of works of fiction was 'Vivian Grey,' published when the author was quite a boy. It has been followed by 'The Young Duke,' 'Contarini Fleming,' 'Henrietta Temple,' 'Venetia,' 'Tancred,' 'Alroy,' 'Ixion,' 'Sybil,' 'Coningsby,' and 'Lothair.'

'Vivian Grey' at once seized the attention of the town, and its successors maintained, if they did not increase, the reputation of the author. They have all been very popular, have been many times reprinted, and sold at all prices, from the conventional guinea and a half form down to the popular 'Companion Library' edition, at a shilling a novel.

Mr. Disraeli comes of an old Jewish family; and the pedigrees of such families are of a length compared with which those of the princes of the blood of any of our European reigning families become insignificant.

His grandfather, Benjamin Disraeli, settled in England in 1748. He was an Italian descendant from one of those Hebrew families whom the Inquisition forced to emigrate from the Spanish Peninsula at the end of the fifteenth century. His ancestors, who were of the Sephardim, 'had dropped their Gothic surname' on their settlement in Italy; 'and, grateful to the God of Jacob, who had sustained them through unprecedented trials and guarded them through unheard-of perils, they assumed the name of DISRAELI —a name never borne before or since by any other family—in order that their race might for ever be recognised.' For two centuries they were merchants at Venice; but England offering many advantages, in the middle of the eighteenth century the present Mr. Disraeli's great-grandfather deter-

THE ARISTOCRACY OF NATURE.

mined on sending his younger son, Benjamin, to settle in this country of political quiet, and civil and religious freedom. This first of the English Disraelis is described by his distinguished grandson as a man 'of ardent character; sanguine, courageous, speculative, and fortunate; with a temper which no disappointment could disturb, and a brain amid reverses full of resource.' No wonder, then, that at middle age he had made a fortune, and settled in a country house at Enfield, where he entertained Sir Horace Mann and many celebrities of the day. He died in 1817, at the ripe age of ninety, and left one son, who had 'disappointed all his plans, and who, to the last hour of his life, was an enigma to him.' This was Isaac Disraeli, the father of the future Prime Minister, and the famous author of 'The Curiosities of Literature' and kindred works—books that will live long after his son's works of fiction have lost their ephemeral glory.

Isaac was of course designed by his father for a merchant; but having written a poem, he was consigned to his father's correspondent at Amsterdam, like a bale of goods, to be placed at a college there. On his return to England, at the age of eighteen, his genius broke the bonds of parental control. He wrote a long poem against Commerce, which—strange sentiment in the mouth of his race as we know them—he called the corrupter of man. He packed up his effusion, and took it to the emperor of the world of letters, Dr. Johnson. Young Isaac Disraeli left it himself in the hands of the Doctor's negro, at the door of the house in Bolt-court, Fleet-street; but the Doctor was then too ill to read anything, and it was returned to the author a week after.

From this time Isaac Disraeli began to lead the life of a student. He was fortunate in making the acquaintance of amiable and cultivated men, who introduced him to congenial society.

His marriage did not alter his recluse habits of life: he continued to live almost entirely in his own library. This gentleman, having had some difference with his synagogue, failed to teach Judaism to the future Prime Minister; and Samuel Rogers, the banker poet, finding the boy, at six years old, without any religious instruction, took him to Hackney church. From that time Mr. Disraeli has been a member of the Church of England. Though born of Jewish parents, he has never held the Jewish faith, but has been all his life a member of the Christian Church. Indeed, his father, Isaac Disraeli, was buried in the chancel of the village church, near his own seat in Buckinghamshire; so it would appear that, if he had made no formal profession of any change of religion, he died a Christian.

Mr. Disraeli, in his youth, was articled to a firm of attorneys, who carried on business in Old Jewry, in the city of London; but he did not remain to complete the term for which he was articled. His genius pointed to greater things; and until he himself contradicted the report, when Mr. Grant's 'History of the Newspaper Press' appeared, it had always been supposed that he had devoted some considerable time at this period of his life to writing for the newspapers. This, however, was a mistake. Mr. Disraeli must be allowed to know best; and it appears that his first literary effort was 'Vivian Grey.' Though the style is turgid, there are strong outbursts of imagination in the novel. 'Books,' says the author, 'written by boys, which pretend to give a picture of manners, and to deal in knowledge of human nature, can be at the best but the results of imagination, acting upon knowledge not acquired by experience.' This sentence precisely describes the character of his first novel. Yet, read by the light of events which have come to pass since he wrote it, 'Vivian Grey' is very full of interest. The hero is so like the author, that it is not easy to separate them. 'Mankind, then,' says Vivian Grey, 'is my game. At this moment, how many a powerful noble only wants wit to be a Minister; and what wants Vivian Grey to attain the same end? That noble's influence.' And, in due time, the creator of 'Vivian' became a Minister; for in February 1852, Lord Derby made Mr. Disraeli his Chancellor of the Exchequer, an office he held a second time when Lord Derby was made Premier in 1858-9; and a third time he filled the office under his veteran friend and leader in 1866. As everybody knows, in 1868, in the month of February, Lord Derby's health compelled him to resign, and her Majesty was pleased to send for Mr. Disraeli, who thus had conferred upon him the crowning distinction of his life, the greatest post the Sovereign has it in her power to bestow.

But Mr. Disraeli did not find his way into the House he was afterwards to lead without a fight for his seat. In 1829, after the very rapid production of his earlier novels, the brilliant young littérateur left England, spent the winter in Constantinople, and visited Syria, Egypt, and Nubia, before his return in 1831. He came back with new views of life and politics. He had penetrated the Asian Mystery, and was something between a Tory and a Whig. Recommended by Hume and O'Connell, he tried Wycombe three times for a seat in Parliament, and was unsuccessful. Then he turned up at Taunton, and discovered himself, what he is now, a Conservative; and in the ardour of his electioneering eloquence attacked the Irish demagogue.

Politics ran higher then than now, and O'Connell replied: 'Mr. Disraeli calls me traitor: my answer to that is that he is a liar. He is a liar in action and in words. His life is a living lie.' This was not quite strong enough. He went on: 'When I speak of Mr. Disraeli as a Jew, I mean not to taunt him on that account. Better ladies and gentleman than amongst the Jews I have never met with. They were once the chosen people of God. There were miscreants among them, however; and it must certainly have been from one of those that Disraeli descended. He possesses just the qualities of the impenitent thief who died upon the Cross, whose name must have been Disraeli. For aught I know, the present Disraeli is descended from him; and, with the impression that he is, I now forgive the heir-at-law of the blasphemous thief that died upon the Cross.'

O'Connell's coarse wit stopped at nothing; but he had a foeman worthy of his steel in the younger Disraeli, as he was called then. O'Connell was bound by a vow not to fight a duel; and Disraeli called upon the son of the demagogue to assume 'his vicarious duties of yielding satisfaction for the insults which his father lavished with impunity on his political opponents.'

Morgan O'Connell did not accept the challenge; and Disraeli wrote Daniel O'Connell a letter, in which he said:

'Although you have long since placed yourself out of the pale of civilisation, still I am one that will not be insulted even by a Yahoo without chastising IT. . . . I called upon your son to assume his vicarious office of yielding satisfaction for his shrinking sire. I admire your scurrilous allusions to my origin. . . You say that I was once a Radical and am now a Tory. My conscience acquits me of ever having deserted a political friend, or of ever having changed a political opinion. I have nothing to appeal to but the good sense of the people. A death's head and cross bones were not blazoned on my banners.'

He called the great demagogue a 'big beggarman,' who gathered 'rint' from the wretched Irish peasantry by promising to procure a 'repale' for them, which he knew he should never get.

Altogether, Mr. Disraeli had much the best of the correspondence. Few men could write a better letter of accusation or of vindication; and he has been charged with the authorship of the 'Runnymede' letters, which appeared in the 'Times.' They are inferior to the letters of 'Junius,' but they display great powers of invective; and, on internal evidence only, most people would say they were written by Disraeli.

Mr. Disraeli first sat in Parliament for Maidstone, in 1832; and his speeches are, perhaps, the best efforts of his genius. He is a splendid Parliamentary debater, and a perfect master of epigrammatic phrases that stick wherever they are applied. When he wrote 'Tancred,' it was his opinion that 'we sadly lack a new stock of public images. The current similes, if not absolutely counterfeit, are quite worn out. They have no intrinsic value, and serve only as counters to represent the absence of ideas. The critics should really call them in.' No man has done more to replace the old images with new ones than the author of 'Tancred.' Perhaps 'Tancred' is the best book of imagination, and 'Coningsby' of political life, that their author has produced. The style of all his novels is sparkling and clever sometimes, at others turgid and over-daubed with colour.

It is curious that the best specimen of Disraeli's style that can be given in a few lines is not Disraeli's at all, but Thackeray's. In his 'Novels by Eminent Hands,' he has 'Codlingsby: by the Right Hon. B. Shrewsberry'—a wonderfully good imitation in caricature of Disraeli's style.

They entered a moderate-sized apartment—indeed Holywell-street is not above a hundred yards long, and this chamber was not more than half that length—and fitted up with the simple taste of its owner.

The carpet was of white velvet—laid over several webs of Aubusson, Ispahan, and Axminster, so that your foot gave no more sound as it trod upon the yielding plain than the shadow which followed you—of white velvet painted with flowers, arabesques, and classic figures by Sir William Ross, J. M. W. Turner, R.A., Mrs. Mee, and Paul Delaroche. The edges were wrought with seed-pearl, Valenciennes lace, and bullion. The walls were hung with cloth of silver, embroidered with gold figures, over which were worked pomegranates, polyanthuses, and passion-flowers, in ruby, amethyst, and smaragd. The drops of dew which the artificers had sprinkled on the flowers were of diamonds. The hangings were overhung with pictures yet more costly. Giorgione the gorgeous, Titian the golden, Rubens the ruddy and pulpy (the Pan of painting), some of Murillo's beatified shepherdesses, who smile on you out of darkness like a star; a few score of first-class Leonardos, and fifty of the masterpieces of the patron of Julius and Leo, the imperial genius of Urbino, covered the walls of the little chamber. Divans of carved amber, covered with ermine, went round the room, and in the midst was a fountain pattering and babbling into jets of double-distilled otto of roses.

'Pipes, Goliath!' Rafael said gaily, to a little negro with a silver collar (he spoke to him in his native tongue of Dongola); 'and welcome to our snuggery, my Codlingsby.'

* * * * * *

Her hair had that deep glowing tinge in it which has been the delight of all painters, and which therefore the vulgar sneer at. It was of burning auburn, meandering over her fairest shoulders in twenty thousand minute ringlets; it hung to her waist, and below it. A light-blue velvet fillet, clasped with a diamond aigrette, valued at two hundred thousand tomauns, and bought from Lieutenant Vicovich, who had received it from Dost Mahomet, with a simple bird of Paradise, formed her head-gear. A sea-green cymar, with short sleeves, displayed her exquisitely-moulded arms to perfection, and was fastened by a girdle of emeralds over a yellow-satin frock. Pink-gauze trousers, spangled with silver, and slippers of the same colour as the band which clasped her ringlets (but so covered with pearls, that the original hue of the charming papoosh disappeared entirely), completed her costume. She had three necklaces on, each of which would have dowered a princess; her fingers glittered with rings to their rosy tips; and priceless bracelets, bangles, and armlets wound round an arm that was whiter than the ivory grand-piano on which it leaned.

Compare Thackeray's admirable caricature with Disraeli's own serious production:

A fountain rose in the centre of the quadrangle, which was surrounded by arcades. Ranged round this fountain, in a circle, were twenty saddled steeds of the highest race, each held by a groom, and each attended by a man-at-arms. All pressed their hands to their hearts as the Emir entered, but with a gravity of countenance which was never for a moment disturbed. Whether their presence were habitual, or only for the occasion, it was unquestionably impressive. Here the travellers dismounted, and Fakredeen ushered Tancred through a variety of saloons, of which the furniture, though simple, as becomes the East, was luxurious, and, of its kind, superb; floors of mosaic marbles, bright carpets, arabesque ceilings, walls of carved cedar, and broad divans of the richest stuffs of Damascus.

'And this divan is for you,' said Fakredeen, showing Tancred into a chamber, which opened upon a flower-garden, shaded by lemon trees. 'I am proud of my mirror,' he added, with some exultation, as he called Tancred's attention to a large French looking-glass, the only one in Lebanon. 'And this,' added Fakredeen, leading Tancred through a suite of marble chambers, this is your bath.'

In the centre of one chamber, fed by a perpetual fountain, was a large alabaster basin, the edges of which were strewn with flowers just culled. The chamber was entirely of porcelain; a golden flower on a ground of delicate green.

'I will send your people to you,' said Fakredeen, 'but in the mean time there are attendants here, who are, perhaps, more used to the duty;' and so saying, he clapped his hands, and several servants appeared bearing baskets of curious linen, whiter than the snow of Lebanon, and a variety of robes.'

And this passage is equalled by hundreds of others profusely strewn through all his works.

You feel, all the while you are reading his books, that the author is laughing at you. There is an air of insincerity about them all; there is not a passage in one of the romances that ever moved the passions of a boarding-school miss. They are very unreal, and very clever; but with all the splendour and wealth of his Eastern imagination, Mr. Disraeli has a fine sense of genuine English humour. What is finer in this way than the talk of the two servants, Mr. Freeman and Mr. Trueman, that Tancred takes with him to Palestine? They are so inimitably true as portraits of the English upper servant.

When Tancred's life is in danger in an Arab encampment where he is wounded and a prisoner, they come in a great state to explain that they don't know how his boots are to be blacked, for in the night these savages have drunk up all the blacking. On another occasion they go to stay at a 'superb Saracenic castle.'

It strikes Freeman and Trueman thus:

'This is the first gentleman's seat I've seen since we left England,' said Freeman.

'There must have been a fine coming of age here,' rejoined Trueman.

'As for that,' replied Freeman, 'comings of age depend in a manner upon meat and drink. They ain't in noways to be carried out with coffee and pipes. Without oxen roasted whole, and broached hogsheads, they ain't in a manner legal.'

The servants' Paradise is meat and drink in England or in Palestine, and Tancred's gentlemen were sorely tried with the coffee and pipes.

They are at a great feast at the castle, when the following conversation occurs:

'And the most curious thing,' said Freeman to Trueman, as they established themselves under a pine-tree, with an ample portion of roast meat, and armed with their travelling knives and forks —'and the most curious thing is, that they say these people are Christians! Who ever heard of Christians wearing turbans?'

'Or eating without knives and forks?' added Trueman.

'It would astonish their weak minds in the steward's room at Bellamont, if they could see all this, John,' said Mr. Freeman pensively. 'A man who travels has very great advantages.'

'And very great hardships too,' said Trueman. 'I don't care for work, but I do like to have my meals regular.'

'This is not bad picking, though,' said Mr. Freeman; 'they call it gazelle, which I suppose is the foreign for venison.'

'If you called this venison at Bellamont,' said Trueman, 'they would look very queer in the steward's room.'

'Bellamont is Bellamont, and this place is this place, John,' said Mr. Freeman. 'The Hameer is a noble gentleman, every inch of him, and I am very glad my lord has got a companion of his own kidney. It is much better than monks and hermits, and low people of that sort, who are not by no means fit company for somebody I could mention, and might turn him into a Papist into the bargain.'

'That would be a bad business,' said Trueman; 'my lady could never abide that. It would be better that he should turn Turk.'

'I am not sure it wouldn't,' said Mr. Freeman. 'It would be in a manner more constitutional. The Sultan of Turkey may send an Ambassador to our Queen, but the Pope of Rome may not.'

'I should not like to turn Turk,' said Trueman, very thoughtfully.

'I know what you are thinking of, John,' said Mr. Freeman, in a serious tone. 'You are thinking if anything were to happen to either of us in this heathen land, where we should get Christian burial.'

'Lord love you, Mr. Freeman, no I wasn't. I was thinking of a glass of ale.'

'Ah!' sighed Freeman, 'it softens the heart to think of such things away from home, as we are. Do you know, John, there are times when I feel very queer—there are indeed. I catched myself a singing "Sweet Home" one night, among those savages in the wilderness. One wants consolation, John, sometimes—one does, indeed; and, for my part, I do miss the family prayers and the home-brewed.'

No author has ever done better in portraying the characteristic feeling of the servants' hall; and at the other social extreme, Mr. Disraeli has had more practice than any other novelist. He has put more dukes, duchesses, lords, and ladies, more gold and jewels, more splendour and wealth into his books than anybody else has attempted to do. They are full of them. They are full, too, of his peculiar opinions about the race from which he has sprung. 'Race,' he tells us, 'is the only truth.' 'The Jews are the aristocracy of nature—the purest race, the chosen people.'

Whatever fate his fame as a statesman and a novelist may meet with at the hands of the future, there is, then, one thing at least he can never lose —his connection with the aristocracy of nature.

JOHN HOLLINGSHEAD.

For fifteen years Mr. Hollingshead has been an active literary and public man. His literary career was begun much later than that of several of his contemporaries, but by his industry and ability he speedily succeeded in placing himself in the van. And in that particular walk of life to which he has devoted his energies, he may be placed in the first rank.

John Hollingshead was born in London in September 1829. He is the son of Mr. Henry Randall Hollingshead; and being intended by his father for a City life, he was educated with this end in view at Homerton. His family have been connected for many generations with City and business circles, and at an early age Mr. Hollingshead was placed with a London firm. But his literary tastes were so strong that he decided to embark on what is to ninety-nine aspirants out of a hundred the frailest bark that ever was launched—literary pursuits.

Having left his desk and the Gillott of commerce, he took up the quill of the man of letters; and when only twenty-six years of age, he had made such headway that his performances strongly recommended him to the late Charles Dickens, who engaged him permanently for the staff of 'Household Words.' Mr. Hollingshead was also a contributor to many leading papers, magazines, and reviews,—among which we may mention the 'Daily News,' 'London Review,' 'Punch,' 'Athenæum,' 'Times of India,' 'Cornhill Magazine,' 'All the Year Round,' and to the columns of 'Once a Week.' Mr. Hollingshead was—we suppose is—a philosophical Radical, and in all the publications he wrote for he religiously preserved his political consistency. He was the devoted disciple of J. Bentham when that worthy was neglected. He can now see Jeremy's image every time he walks on the pavement in front of the façade of Burlington House. Many of Mr. Hollingshead's most successful papers were written with the intention of making popular the principles of Mill and Bentham; and it appears that

SO HE PLAYS HIS PART. *As You like it*, act ii. sc. 7.

though the great humorist had little sympathy with the school himself, he let his collaborateur say what he liked on the subject in 'All the Year Round.'

In 1859 some of his most popular papers were first collected and published in separate form, with the title of 'Under Bow Bells.' This volume contained the well-known essay called 'The City of Unlimited Paper,' which had attracted a great deal of attention in the monetary panic of 1857.

'Rubbing the Gilt off,' which appeared in 1860, was a collection of clever political essays, written in a very lively style—very readable, even to people who do not care about politics—and dedicated to John Bright, at a time when the ex-Cabinet Minister had apparently about as much chance of being made Archimandrite as President of the Board of Trade.

This book was followed by a collection of travels entitled 'Odd Journeys,' and by a volume of humorous papers entitled 'Ways of Life.' In the same year (1861) 'Ragged London' appeared. This was the reproduction of a series of letters which were published originally in the 'Morning Post.' The author's other publications are a collection of humorous stories entitled 'Rough Diamonds,' and two volumes of miscellaneous essays called 'To-day.'

Mr. Hollingshead is likewise a successful dramatist; and when the Exhibition of 1862 was projected he was called upon by the Commissioners to write the historical introduction to the official catalogues—work done in 1851 by Mr. Cole, C.B.

In 1866, in connection with Mr. Dion Boucicault, he had carried through an agitation which resulted in dramatic free trade; and the attention of capitalists having been drawn to the want of first-class theatres in London, several have been built since that date. The Gaiety Theatre, in the Strand, is the best and most successful of the new theatres. Mr. Hollingshead opened it in December 1868, and is still lessee and manager of this, one of the most popular of our London playhouses. He has so played his part as manager as to please every taste, and has always secured the services of a first-rate company. His new dramas have been written by Robertson, Charles Reade, Gilbert, Oxenford, Byron, and Boucicault; and his company has included the names of Toole, Wigan, Boucicault, Charles Mathews, Mrs. Boucicault, Miss Neilson, and Miss Farren.

A. C. SWINBURNE.

Mr. Swinburne, who was born at Holmwood in Surrey in 1843, received his education at Eton and Oxford. He left the University without taking a degree, and in 1861 published his first poems—'The Queen Mother,' and 'Rosamond.'

These first efforts were not received with much favour either by the critics or by the general public; but, four years afterwards, the publication of 'Atalanta in Calydon' at once placed the young and ardent poet in the first rank among our living bards.

He was enabled to dispute the laurels with Browning and Tennyson. The feeling and inspiration of the 'Atalanta' are thoroughly Greek, and it is written in rich yet simple English, artfully elaborated into most liquid verse.

There is no poet whose verses are more beautifully liquid and flowing than Mr. Swinburne's, and this quality is quite distinctive of him. His power of rhyming is wonderful. 'Sestina,' the poem published in the early part of 1872, bears witness to this, as there are only two rhymes all through it.

Subsequently to the publication of 'Atalanta in Calydon,' Mr. Swinburne produced (in 1865) 'Poems and Ballads.' However beautiful many of the poems in this volume were, their charm was destroyed by others which were neither wholesome nor good.

Of late, Mr. Swinburne has turned over a new leaf, and all his recently published verses are as unobjectionable in matter as they are poetic in inspiration and finished in execution. Whatever else may be urged against Mr. Swinburne's writings, it can never be denied that they are the productions of a true poet.

A TRUE POET.

H

J. C. M. BELLEW.

John Chippendale Montesquieu Bellew is the only son of the late Captain Robert Higgin, of Lancaster. He was born in 1823. His mother was a member of the family of Lord Bellew, in Ireland; and he has assumed his mother's maiden name. He was educated at the Grammar School, Lancaster, and entered at St. Mary's Hall, Oxford, in 1842. Here he became a regular speaker at the Union Debating Society, and in 1848 he was ordained a curate at St. Andrew's, Worcester. In 1850, he became curate at Prescot, whence he went out to the East Indies as a chaplain in the following year. He was attached to St. John's Cathedral, Calcutta, from that date till 1855, when he returned to England, and undertook a temporary engagement at St. Philip's, Regent-street. Here he gained great celebrity for his powers of oratory; and, after having held some temporary clerical appointments, he became in 1862 incumbent of Bedford Chapel, Bloomsbury.

Mr. Bellew is the author of a novel entitled 'Blount Tempest,' 'The History of Holland House,' and other works.

Some four years since, Mr. Bellew retired from the incumbency of Bedford Chapel, and embraced the Catholic faith.

As a skilful elocutionist and successful reader, Mr. Bellew is in all probability without a rival; and he excels alike in humorous and pathetic pieces, as all who have had the pleasure of listening to him in two such entirely opposite pieces as 'Horatius' and 'The Charity Dinner' can testify. It may be questioned if any single reader has ever succeeded in gathering together such large and appreciative audiences as Mr. Bellew; and his popularity, instead of being on the wane, appears to increase daily. Personally, Mr. Bellew is a handsome man, with a commanding presence—natural gifts which he turns to the greatest advantage on the platform.

MASTER OF ONE OF THE 'THREE Rs'

Doubtless, he owes no inconsiderable portion of his success to his hair, which he wears in a most melodramatic fashion.

He has distanced all his competitors in his own line—which is that of giving theatrical renderings of the best writers to a very worthy class of people, who would never think of entering the doors of a playhouse.

His best humorous readings—'Love in a Balloon' and 'The Charity Dinner'—are published in 'Once a Week.' Years ago, Mr. Bellew proved himself to be a master of one of the three Rs—reading. His reputation has been fairly earned.

HENRY IRVING.

'The Bells' was produced by Mr. Bateman on the 25th of November 1871, and the critics were unanimous in their praise of the acting of the principal character of the piece. Indeed, the play is essentially a one-part piece—as completely so as 'Leah' is. It is founded on the story of 'The Polish Jew,' by those great novelists, MM. Erckmann-Chatrian—the twin brothers of modern French romance.

The play is adapted by Mr. Leopold Lewis, who seems to have performed the task of taking other men's ideas as well as adapters generally. His version of 'The Polish Jew' opens as 'The Corsican Brothers' does— with a narrative of the motive incident of the plot.

Mathias keeps an inn in Alsace. In the common room of this inn, Walter and Hans are talking of the murder of the Polish Jew, which happened fifteen years before; when Mathias, the rich innkeeper, returns from a visit to Paris. Mathias was the murderer. He is astonished and alarmed to find the crime still a topic of conversation. When he killed the Jew for the gold he carried in his belt, he was poor and embarrassed. Now he is wealthy and prosperous, and the chief man in the village. His daughter is to be married to Christian, and he can give her a dowry of thirty thousand francs.

In Paris he has seen a mesmerist put people into the mesmeric sleep, and make them disclose their thoughts. This has made a deep impression on his mind. He sups; drinks with Hans and Walter; and after they are gone, is alone with his disordered fancy. The sledge bells ring again in his ears; again he sees the face of the murdered Jew; the soughing wind blows back on him the Jew's blessing, 'God be with you!' Still the sledge bells ring, and Mathias sees his victim driving in the snow. With a wild and terrible cry, he faints and falls.

In the second act he is hurrying on the signing of the marriage contract.

MATHIAS.

But as he writes his name to the parchment, the bells ring in his ears, each chime a fiendish voice to rack his soul.

The deed is signed, and witnessed by half the village. They dance a dance of joy. Mathias, leaping up, joins in it, and shouts and sings with a mad glee.

In the third act the guests depart, and Mathias resolves to sleep alone; for he talks in his sleep. He locks the door of his chamber, and retires to his bed—to dream; and, in his dream, to live again through all his night of crime. But with a new horror. A prisoner at the bar, he fancies the mesmerist makes him sleep, and tell his judges, with his own lips, the secret story of his guilt.

Day comes. His wife and Christian break open the door of his chamber. They lift Mathias from his bed of horrors, in a dying state. He breathes his last in their arms.

Such is the plot of 'The Bells.'

Of Mr. Irving's character of Mathias, it is impossible to speak too highly. It is the finest impersonation seen on the English stage for years. It is a work of the highest art. The actor is lost in his creation. You see only Mathias, the terror-stricken murderer. The acting in the dream scene can only be charged with one fault. It is too real, too terrible. And at the end, the presentment of death is perfect.

Mr. Irving appeared first on the London stage, nearly six years ago, in a play called 'The Belles' Stratagem,' at the Theatre Royal, St. James's.

CHARLES READE.

Mr. Charles Reade is the youngest son of the late John Reade, Esquire, of Ipsden House, Oxfordshire. Mr. Reade is an Oxford man (he took his B.A. degree in 1835), and is a Doctor of Civil Law, and a fellow of Magdalen College in that university. He was called to the bar by the Honourable Society of Lincoln's Inn in 1843.

Charles Reade's earliest stories were followed in 1856 by that powerful work of his genius, 'It is Never too Late to Mend.' The book created a great sensation: was read by everybody: and effected its author's purpose—viz. compelled the public to insist that the Model Prisons' system should be looked searchingly into.

From the publication of 'Peg Woffington,' Charles Reade has continued to apply his great talents to the work of writing novels and dramas: with what success, every reader of fiction knows.

The annexed complete list of his writings will give a correct idea of the extent of his productions in the difficult field of the Literature of Imagination, in which he has chosen to exercise his genius.

Stories in order of production.

	VOLS.		VOLS.
Peg Woffington	1	Eighth Commandment	1
Christie Johnstone	1	The Cloister and the Hearth	4
Clouds and Sunshine ⎫		Hard Cash	3
Propria quæ Maribus ⎬	1	Griffith Gaunt	3
Art ⎭		Foul Play†	3
It is Never too Late to Mend	3	Put Yourself in his Place	3
Love me Little, Love me Long	2	A Terrible Temptation	3
Autobiography of a Thief ⎫ *	1	A Simpleton.	
Jack of all Trades ⎭		Graphic Christmas Supplement.	
White Lies	3		

* Under title of 'Cream.' † With Dion Boucicault.

SOMETHING LIKE A NOVELIST.

Dramas in order of production.

The Ladies' Battle	Translation.
The Village Tale	Three-act drama.
The Lost Husband	Four-act drama.
Masks and Faces*	Two-act comedy.
Gold	Drama, five acts.
Two Loves and a Life*	Drama, four acts.
The King's Rival*	Comedy, five acts.
The First Printer*	Drama, three acts.
The Courier of Lyons	Drama, three acts.
Honour before Titles	Drama, three acts.
It is Never too Late to Mend	Drama, five acts.
Griffith Gaunt	Drama, five acts.
Foul Play	Drama, five acts.
Dora	Pastoral drama, three acts.
The Double Marriage	Drama, five acts.
Put Yourself in his Place	Drama, five acts.
The Robust Invalid	Comedy, three acts.
Shilly Shally†	Comedy, three acts.

This list shows that Charles Reade is the author, or joint-author—in four plays and one novel—of nineteen different stories, ranging in length from one-third of a volume to four volumes: and of eighteen dramatic works.

Now it certainly argues some want of real knowledge or study in the critics of the day, that they cannot assign his place, whatever that may be, to this writer. They can place inferior authors, but they really and honestly have no notion where this man stands, either as a novelist, or dramatist, or both. Perhaps it may tend to clear this absolute fog enveloping the judgment of the critics, if we descend from the indefinite to the definite, and compare him with a writer of acknowledged excellence. We are so fortunate as to possess in this country a novelist who, if contemporary criticism were to be trusted, is the greatest writer of fiction the world ever saw. With regard to Shakspeare, contemporary criticism has left but two remarks in print, both of them unfavourable. Corneille was so often lashed, and so little praised, that he has left a line behind him to celebrate the fact:

'J'ai peu des voix pour moi, mais je les ai sans brigue.'

* With Tom Taylor.   † Founded on Trollope's novel.

Molière was denounced as a plagiarist; Voltaire was well lashed; Scott did not quite escape; Bulwer has been severely criticised; even Dickens was always roughly handled in certain respectable prints.

But George Eliot is faultless. This is the sober and often repeated verdict of every quarterly, monthly, and daily critic in the empire, except of one writer, who tried to stem the torrent of adulation in the 'Quarterly Review,' and failed because, being no critic, he selected certain of that excellent writer's beauties, and held them up for faults.

Now perhaps some people will open their eyes if we tell them that this prodigious writer often borrows ideas from Charles Reade, and sometimes improves them, sometimes bungles them. But, as in matters of art it is sometimes kind to open people's eyes, we shall assure you that this is so; and moreover that in a single instance the two writers have come into competition on fair terms, and the comparison is so unfavourable to the favourite, that the said comparison, though obvious, has always been dexterously avoided.

In 'It is Never too Late to Mend,' published in 1856, one of the situations is as follows: Good Mr. Eden, having to deal with a hardened thief, goes down on his knees in that thief's cell, and prays aloud for him; and softens him a little. In 'Adam Bede,' good Dinah goes on her knees in the cell of Hetty, an impenitent criminal; and softens her a little.

Reade uses few words, after his kind; and Eliot uses many words, after her kind. But amplification is not invention: the inventor and the only inventor of that famous scene in 'Adam Bede' is Charles Reade.

Mr. Eden preaches a sermon in the gaol. The author shuns the beaten track, and gives the very words of the sermon.

George Eliot profits by this, and gives her Dinah the very words of a sermon. And in one respect she goes beyond her original: for her sermon is fuller, and has a distinct merit, being composed—with great heart and beauty—of homely English, often Saxon, and nearly always monosyllabic. But she falls behind in one thing—she makes Dinah preach her sermon to strangers; and that shows a want of constructive art.

Charles Reade has since returned to his own invention, and has made his Rhoda Somerset preach a remarkable sermon, at which those personages are present whom that sermon hits. This is art. A sermon, preached to the reader only, is a mere excrescence on the narrative. It is a wart, though it may not be a blot.

The only situation of any power in 'The Mill on the Floss'—viz. the heroine and her lover drifting loose in a boat, and being out together all night—is manifestly taken from the similar situation in 'Love me Little, Love me Long.' But Eliot's treatment of the borrowed incident is petty and womanish by comparison with her model.

In 'Felix Holt,' the ground is admirably laid for strong situations: but in the actual treatment only two come out dramatically, and they are both borrowed. The young gentleman going to strike his steward, and being met by 'I am your Father;' and the heroine going into the witness-box to give evidence for her lover. The former is borrowed from an old novel, and the latter from Charles Reade's 'Hard Cash;' and it may be instructive to show how the inventor and the imitator deal with the idea.

We print in parallel columns quotations of the evidence given in court by both novelists' heroines.

HARD CASH. (Vol. iii. p. 294, 1863.) BY CHARLES READE.	FELIX HOLT THE RADICAL. (Vol. iii. p. 228, 1866.) BY GEORGE ELIOT.
Julia Dodd entered the box, and a sunbeam seemed to fill the court. She knew what to do: her left hand was gloved, but her white right hand bare. She kissed the book; and gave her evidence in her clear, mellow, melting voice: gave it reverently and modestly, for to her the court was a church. She said how long she had been acquainted with Alfred, and how his father was adverse, and her mother had thought it was because they did not pass for rich, and had told her they *were* rich; and with this she produced David's letter, and she also swore to having met Alfred and others carrying her father in a swoon from his father's very door. She deposed to Alfred's sanity on her wedding-eve, and on the day his recapture was attempted. Saunders, against his own judgment, was instructed to cross-examine her; and, without meaning it, he put a question which gave her deep distress.	There was no blush upon her face: she stood, divested of all personal considerations, whether of vanity or shyness. Her clear voice sounded as it might have done if she had been making a confession of faith. She began and went on without query or interruption. Every face looked grave and respectful. 'I am Esther Lyon, the daughter of Mr. Lyon, the Independent minister at Treby, who has been one of the witnesses for the prisoner. I knew

'Are you now engaged to the plaintiff?'

She looked timidly round, and saw Alfred, and hesitated. The serjeant pressed her politely, but firmly.

'Must I reply to that?' she said piteously.

'If you please.'

'Then, no. Another misfortune has now separated him and me for ever.'

'What is that, pray?'

'My father is said to have died at sea; and my mother thinks *he* is to blame.'

The Judge to Saunders.—What on earth has this to do with Hardie against Hardie?

Saunders.—You are warmly interested in the plaintiff's success?

Julia.—O yes, sir.

(*Colt, aside to Garrow.*—The fool is putting his foot into it: there's not a jury in England that would give a verdict to part two interesting young lovers.)

Saunders.—You are attached to him?

Julia.—Ah, that I do!

This burst, intended for poor Alfred, not the court, baffled cross-examination and grammar and everything else. Saunders was wise and generous, and said no more.

Colt cast a glance of triumph, and declined to reëxamine. He always let well alone. The Judge, however, evinced a desire to trace the fourteen thousand pounds from Calcutta; but Julia could not help him: that mysterious sum had been announced by letter as about to sail; and then no more was heard about it till Alfred accused his father of having it. All endeavours to fill this hiatus failed. However Julia, observing that in courts material objects affect the mind most, had provided herself with all the *pièces de conviction* she could find, and she produced her father's empty pocket-book, and said, when he was brought home senseless, this was in his breast-pocket.

'Hand it up to me,' said the Judge. He examined it, and said it had been in the water.

'Captain Dodd was wrecked off the French coast,' suggested Mr. Saunders.

'My learned friend had better go into the witness-box, if he means to give evidence,' said Mr. Colt.

'You are very much afraid of a very little truth,' retorted Saunders.

Felix Holt well. On the day of the election at Treby, when I had been much alarmed by the noises that reached me from the main street, Felix Holt came to call upon me. He knew that my father was away, and he thought that I should be alarmed by the sounds of disturbance. It was about the middle of the day, and he came to tell me that the disturbance was quieted, and that the streets were nearly emptied. But he said he feared that the men would collect again after drinking, and that something worse might happen later in the day. And he was in much sadness at this thought. He stayed a little while, and then he left me. He was very melancholy. His mind was full of great resolutions, that came from his kind feeling towards others. It was the last thing he would have done to join in riot or to hurt any man, if he could have helped it. His nature is very noble: he is tender-hearted; he could never have had any intention that was not brave and good.'

There was something so naïve and beautiful in this action of Esther's, that it conquered every low or petty suggestion even in the commonest minds.

The Judge stopped this sham rencontre, by asking the witness whether her father had been wrecked. She said, 'Yes.'

'And that is how the money was lost,' persisted Saunders.

'Possibly,' said the Judge.

'I'm darned if it was,' said Joshua Fullalove composedly.

Instantly, all heads were turned in amazement at this audacious interruption to the soporific decorum of an English court. The transatlantic citizen received this battery of eyes with complete imperturbability.

Fertile situations are the true cream of fiction; these once supplied, any professional writer can find words.

Now, the fertile situation in 'Felix Holt' was supplied by Charles Reade. The true literary patent is in him. His is the witness with the clear mellow voice who gives her evidence as if before God—and that witness a young lady who loves the man for whom she gives evidence, he being present. To be sure, George Eliot's witness shows a disposition to argue the case; but that is no improvement on the original.

We will now call attention to another instance of George Eliot's imitation of Charles Reade.

In his little story, 'Clouds and Sunshine,' Charles Reade uses this expression—'the thunder of the horses' feet drawing the wagon into the barn.'

His unlucky imitator pounces on his 'thunder' and his 'wagon' and deals with them thus: 'The thunder of the wagon coming up the hill.' Now the iron shoes of a team going over the wooden floor of a barn do come the nearest to thunder of anything we ever heard; but a wagon coming *up* a hill does not thunder; the most prominent sound is the creaking of the slow wheels. This, then, is unintelligent imitation on a smaller scale.

In 1860 Mr. Reade produced a mediæval novel with an idea-ed title, 'The Cloister and the Hearth.'

His faithful imitator soon followed suit with a mediæval novel, whose title was unidea-ed—'Romola.'

Here the two writers met on an arena that tests the highest quality they both pretend to—Imagination.

What is the result? In 'The Cloister and the Hearth' you have the middle ages, long and broad. The story begins in Holland, and the quaint

Dutch figures live; it goes through Germany, and Germany lives; it picks up a French arbalétrier, and the mediæval French soldier is alive again. It goes to Rome, and the Roman men and women live again.

Compare with this the narrow canvas of 'Romola,' and the faint colours. The petty politics of mediæval Florence made to sit up in the grave, but not to come out of it. The gossip of modern Florence turned on to mediæval subjects and called mediæval gossip. Romola herself is a high-minded, delicate-minded, sober-minded lady of the nineteenth century, and no other. She has a gentle but tame and non-mediæval affection for a soft egotist who belongs to that or any age you like. One great historical figure, Savonarola, is taken, and turned into a woman by a female writer: sure sign imagination is wanting. There is a dearth of powerful incidents, though the time was full of them, as 'The Cloister and the Hearth' is full of them. There you have the *broad* features of that marvellous age, so full of grand anomalies: the fine arts and the spirit that fed them; the feasts, the shows, the domestic life, the laws, the customs, the religion; the roads and their perils; the wild beasts disputing the civilised continent with man, man uppermost by day, the beasts by night; the hostelries, the robbers, the strange vows; the convents, shipwrecks, sieges, combats, escapes; a robbers' slaughter-house burnt, and the fire lighting up trees clad with snow. And through all this a deep current of true love—passionate, yet pure—ending in a mediæval poem: the battle of ascetic religion against our duty to our neighbour, which was the great battle of the time that shook religious souls. But perhaps we shall be told this comparison is beside the mark; that a dearth of incidents is better than a surfeit, and that it is in the higher art of drawing characters George Eliot stands supreme, and Charles Reade fills an insignificant place. We will abide by that test in this comparison.

What genuine mediæval characters, to be compared with those of Walter Scott, for instance, live in the memory after reading the two works we are comparing?

'The Cloister and the Hearth' is a gallery of such portraits, painted in full colours to the life. 'Romola' is a portfolio of delicate studies. 'Romola' leaves on the memory: 1, a young lady of the nineteenth century, the exact opposite of a mediæval woman; 2, the soft egotist, an excellent type; 3, an innocent little girl; 4, Savonarola emasculated. The other characters talk nineteen to the dozen, but they are little more than voluble shadows.

'The Cloister and the Hearth' fixes on the mind: 1, the true lover, hermit and priest, Gerard; 2, the true lover, mediæval and northern, Margaret of Sevenbergen; 3, Dame Catherine, economist, gossip, and mother; 4, the dwarf with his big voice; 5, the angelic cripple, little Kate; 6, the Burgomaster; 7, the Burgundian soldier, a character hewn out of mediæval rock; 8, the gaunt Dominican, hard, but holy; 9, the patrician monk, in love with heathenism, but safe from fiery fagots because he believed in the Pope; 10, the patrician Pope, in love with Plutarch, and sated with controversy; 11, the Princess Clælia, a true mediæval; 12, the bravo's wife, a link between ancient and mediæval Rome.

Philip of Burgundy does but cross the scene; yet he leaves his mark. Margaret Van Eyck is but flung upon the broad canvas; yet that single figure so drawn has suggested three volumes to another writer.

You can find a thousand Romolas in London, because she is drawn from observation, and is quite out of place in a mediæval tale. But you cannot find the characters of 'The Cloister and the Hearth,' because they are creations.

When 'The Cloister and the Hearth' was first published, the 'Saturday Review,' staggered by the contents of the book, yet bound by the sacred tie of habit to say something against it, summed it up as inferior on the whole to Walter Scott. But nobody has ever compared 'Romola' to Walter Scott. Adulation, however fulsome, has evaded this comparison, because it would have provoked derision; and no reviewer, until this article was written, ever had the courage to compare 'Romola' with 'The Cloister and the Hearth.' Yet any one who has not made that comparison honestly and fairly knows little of Charles Reade, and cannot possibly assign him his true place amongst living writers of fiction.

Of 'The Cloister and the Hearth' it is impossible to speak too well. The author's perfect knowledge of mediæval life, just before the time of Erasmus, is wonderful. The plot is full of incident of the newest and most striking, yet most probable and natural sort: the characters live, and seem to us real persons we know well: the France, Italy, Holland, and Germany of the time of Erasmus are faithfully reproduced. The interest never flags: there is always something to command attention and excite curiosity. 'The Cloister and the Hearth' is one of the most scholarlike and learned, as well as one of the most artistic and beautiful, works of fiction in any language. This splendid production can only be compared with the best books of one author—Walter Scott. And in all things it is as good as 'Kenilworth' and 'Ivanhoe:' in some points it is better. Although we place two of Charles Reade's books first in their respective classes—'Foul Play' in the class of novels called sensational, and 'The Cloister and the Hearth' in that of the purely imaginative—yet his books, taken throughout, are of more even merit than those of almost any other novelist. They are written in English as pure, as simple, and as truly Saxon as any this century has produced: in a literary style—nervous, vigorous, and masculine—with which the most captious and partisan critic cannot find any fault.

Read him: resign yourself to the magic spell of his genius, and be lifted above the cares of everyday life into the regions of imagination, peopled by his real creations. You may be trusted then to draw your own conclusions as to the merit of his books.

By the million readers of the time to come, Bulwer, Dickens, Thackeray, and Reade will be handed down to fame together in every English-speaking country.

To the scholar and the man of culture, 'The Cloister and the Hearth' may possibly be dearer than the humorous and wonderful creations of Dickens's fertile genius, or the life-like characters and satirical digressions of Thackeray.

TOM HOOD.

Tom Hood, the well-known editor of the comic journal, 'Fun,' son of the late celebrated poet and author, born at Lake House, Wanstead, Essex, January 19, 1835, was educated at University College School and Louth Grammar School, Lincolnshire; entered (intended for the Church) as a commoner at Pembroke College, Oxford, in 1853, where he passed all the examinations for the degree, but did not put on the gown, of B.A. His first work, 'Pen and Pencil Pictures,' written at Oxford, was published in 1854, 5. It was followed by 'Quips and Cranks,' and 'Daughters of King Daher, and other Poems,' in 1861; 'Loves of Tom Tucker and Little Bo-Peep, a Rhyming Rigmarole,' in 1862; 'Vere Vereker's Vengeance, a Sensation,' in 1864; 'Captain Master's Children, a Novel,' and 'Jingles and Jokes for the Little Folks,' in 1865. Novels: 'A Disputed Inheritance,' 'Golden Heart,' 'A Lost Link,' and 'Love and Valour.' He has written several books for juveniles, and illustrated his father's comic verses, 'Precocious Piggy,' having on other occasions wielded pencil as well as pen; and was appointed editor of 'Fun,' which had passed into the hands of a new proprietor, in May 1865. Tom Hood is a contributor to many magazines and periodicals, and has had some experience as a journalist. He is also author of two books on English verse composition. In 1868 he again started the 'Comic Annual,' which has achieved a decided success.

The popularity of 'Fun' under Mr. Hood's care speaks volumes for his skill and judgment as an editor; and he has a recognised position as an author, standing high in public favour.

FUN.

K

BENJAMIN WEBSTER.

This veteran actor had earned a great reputation many years ago. His name will go down to future generations of playgoers as that of one who was a master of the art of embodying on the stage every variety of character. No man has played with success in a greater number of characters than the proprietor of the Adelphi.

Benjamin Webster is descended from a good Yorkshire family, though the city of Bath was his birthplace. He made his first appearance on the stage of life on the 3d of September 1800. He was educated for the navy, and a commission was procured for him by the late Duchess of York; but he never entered the service. The navy has been the loser and the stage the gainer by the circumstance. He was fond of music, and made that his first profession. While fulfilling an engagement in the orchestra of the theatre at Warwick, he first threw down the fiddlestick, and put on the mask and tights of a harlequin—a character different from those with which in after years he pleased the public. But his real début as an actor took place in the same theatre, in the character of Thessalus in 'Alexander the Great.' He succeeded, and resolved to devote himself for the future to the stage. His career after this was that of most young actors. He travelled from town to town, playing all sorts of parts at all sorts of theatres—a training which proved most beneficial. After various adventures in England and Ireland, he turned up in London, where he played trifling parts at several houses. At length, in 1825, 'Measure for Measure' was being performed at Drury Lane, with a strong cast, and Harley had the part of Pompey the clown. The popular comedian was suddenly taken ill. At three or four hours' notice, Benjamin Webster took his place, delighted the audience, pleased the manager, and filled the press with his praises. From this time his name was made. He had plenty of good offers; and in 1829 he opened at the Haymarket, in 'Lodgings for Single Gentlemen.' When Morris, the

THE GOVERNOR.

lessee, retired, Mr. Webster took his place, and for sixteen years was lessee of that house. At the end of that time Mr. Buckstone took it, and Mr. Webster devoted himself exclusively to the Adelphi.

In 1858 he rebuilt that theatre, an old and inconvenient house, and raised in its stead one of the most complete and well-constructed houses in London. The Haymarket owes its position to his energy and liberality. He spent 2000*l*. a-year on English authors at a time when, as now, there was a cry that everything worth seeing was cribbed from the French. Knowles, Bulwer, and Jerrold supplied him with plays; and Macready, Phelps, Wallack, Warde, Farren, Reeve, Buckstone, Charles Mathews, Power, Helen Faucit, Mrs. Glover, Mrs. Warner, and Mrs. Stirling, illustrated them. Not least in this list of 'all the talents' was Benjamin Webster himself. It has been said of him, that 'his motley assumptions remind us of a crowd of Hogarth's. In looking back over all the years of his career, the mass is overpowering. Though each face is individual—old age and youth, fops and vulgarians, Cockneys and countrymen, misers and gamblers, blacklegs and priests; Welshmen, Scotchmen, and Dutchmen; negroes, Jesuits, and Jews—their habiliments would form the wardrobe of a theatre.' Perhaps his greatest impersonation, out of all the characters he assumed, was that of Robert Landry, in the 'Dead Heart.' This was a wonderful delineation of character; and the scene in which Robert recovers his memory, after many years' incarceration in the Bastille, is as fine a piece of acting as ever was seen on the English stage. Old playgoers, too, will recall with delight his George Darville, his Richard Pride, and his Tartuffe. In all his characters, he entered heart and soul into the author's meaning, and the spectator was lost in the reality of the scene.

One other feature of Mr. Webster's career deserves notice; it is his connection with the Royal Dramatic College. This valuable institution he has from the first assisted with his purse and his labour, and has always done all he could to help it on to its present usefulness to decayed members of the profession.

Mr. Webster's very long connection with the stage has caused him to be looked upon as a sort of Nestor among actors; his friends, private and professional, looking up to him as 'the Governor.'

ANTHONY TROLLOPE.

The name of Trollope was as familiar to the last generation of readers as it is to the present. Mrs. Fanny Trollope—she married in 1809 Anthony Trollope, barrister-at-law—having lost her husband, applied herself to literature. In 1832, the year of the Reform Bill in England, she published her first book. It was about the United States, where she had lived for some time, and was called 'Domestic Life of the Americans.'

In England, it was read and enjoyed. In the States, the people did not like it—they did not appear to advantage in the book; but it made the reputation of the lady who had written it; and Mrs. Fanny Trollope continued to apply herself to the manufacture of interesting and clever books, her chef-d'œuvre being 'The Widow Barnaby.' The authoress died at Florence in 1863; and in the outskirts of that city her eldest son, Thomas Adolphus Trollope, has made his home.

Her second son, the subject of this notice, has made England his home, and the English people his study.

Anthony Trollope seems to have 'thrown back' one generation. His grandfather was a parson; and it is in delineating the phases of clerical life, from the bishop to the curate, that this popular writer excels. Bishop Proudie, Archdeacon Grantley, the Rev. Obadiah Slope, Mr. Crawley of Hogglestock, are creations of his genius that have their originals in life. They are photographic portraits of men his readers know: nature clothed with the form of art: and from this exquisite truthfulness they derive their interest.

The conversations of the characters in his books are exactly the dialogues one hears in everyday life. One man turns to Trollope for his recreation, because 'it is exactly like life, you know.' Another man says: 'When I pick up a novel, I want to be taken above everyday life. I want the ideal. I don't find this in Trollope.' And so he does not read Trollope's

TO PARSONS GAVE UP, WHAT WAS MEANT FOR MANKIND.

books. These readers are types: the realist loving reality, which he finds; the idealist seeking for the noble, unselfish, poetic, which he does not find. Trollope's point of view is real and perfectly natural, but it is low.

His parsons, whether they are bishops, prebendaries, deans, vicars, or curates, are, as a rule, the selfish men of everyday life. Their wives are more worldly and selfish than they. What, then, is the mission of the novelist—to educate or to depict? The numerous readers of the popular author must answer this.

Literary fame is a thing of slow growth, generally. Anthony Trollope began with a story, historical and dull, entitled 'La Vendée,' published by Colburn in 1850. He had missed his mark, but he soon rectified the mistake. In 1855 he published 'The Warden,' being the history of the Rev. Septimus Harding, warden of Hiram's Hospital, in the city of Barchester. Two years later, 'Barchester Towers' appeared; in 1858, 'Dr. Thorne,' another story of churchmen; and in the same year, 'The Three Clerks,' a story of legal and political life. In 1859, the prolific pen of the author furnished Mudie's subscribers with 'The Bertrams,' and an Irish story, 'The Kellys and the O'Kellys.' In the next year (1860), 'Castle Richmond' made its appearance; and then Thackeray invited Mr. Trollope to open the ball in 'The Cornhill' with a new story. This story, 'Framley Parsonage,' is one of his best productions. It is a charming piece of genre painting in ink, and did its part in maintaining his reputation, if it did not add anything to it. 'Orley Farm' (1862), 'Rachel Ray' (1863), 'The Small House at Allington,' and 'Can you forgive her?' followed in 1864, almost together; 'Miss Mackenzie' in '65, and 'The Belton Estate' in '66. In '67, 'The Last Chronicle of Barset,' and 'The Claverings;' in '69, 'He knew he was right,' and 'Phineas Finn.' 'The Vicar of Bulhampton,' 'Sir Harry Hotspur of Humblethwaite,' 'Ralph the Heir,' and 'The Golden Lion of Granpere,' close the list.

What other novelist has written as many stories of even merit? They are all below the high mark of the great writers; but all are interesting, all show good sound art in their manipulation. They represent a great total of work conscientiously performed. It seems well, in these fast times, to keep the ball rolling. Mrs. Henry Wood, Miss Braddon, and Anthony

Trollope have laid this truth to heart. They have all of them a public, and they always take care to provide amusement for their readers. Something of theirs is always 'going on somewhere.'

This policy is sound. Fashions and tastes change, new writers may spring up, or old ones wear out. They charm while they may, while their 'copy' has a market value, and act on that most excellent proverb of making their hay while the sun shines. It is well that they should do so; and nobody's hay, old or new, is sweeter in the mouth than that of the writer whose books we have named. He is an artist who goes to nature for his materials; whose puppets are flesh and blood, not clothes-horses; and against whom the only fault we have to bring is, that he has, perhaps, too much 'to parsons given up what was meant for mankind.'

C. E. MUDIE.

CHARLES EDWARD MUDIE, the subject of our cartoon, was born October 18, 1818, at Cheyne-walk, Chelsea, where his father kept a small library, old-fashioned, but good of its kind, and well frequented by the literary dwellers in that then fashionable suburb. Some of our older readers may, perhaps, still remember the little lad attending at his father's counter, too young in the business to do more than fetch and carry, but already a diligent reader of all the books within his reach.

The elder Mudie relinquished the Cheyne-walk library in 1828, and removed with his family to Coventry-street, where he commenced a stationery business, still carried on by one of his sons. There young Charles Edward remained for a few years, spending most of his time in reading what works of philosophy and history he could manage to procure. In those days it was difficult to find a library from which it was possible, at a moderate cost, to obtain any books better worth reading than the ordinary novels of the period; and there was, therefore, nothing for it in his case but to buy the books he could not borrow. In this way he, in the course of time, accumulated a considerable collection of standard works.

One morning, in the spring of 1840, the idea occurred to young Mudie that there were many readers who, like himself, experienced this difficulty in procuring the higher class of books, and who would gladly patronise an undertaking which would place the better literature within their reach. Acting upon this idea, he commenced business in Southampton-row—then Upper King-street, Bloomsbury—by placing the whole of his collection in a window, with a printed intimation of his purpose, under the now familiar title of 'Mudie's Select Library.' The 'select' library soon attracted a select circle of readers, and as this circle enlarged the supply of books increased; until, in the course of a few years, the success of the enterprise was so well assured that the proprietor ventured to advance from tens to

BOOKS.

hundreds, and finally to thousands, of copies of works of high repute and worth; of Livingstone's travels, for example, 3250 copies were taken on the day of publication.

In 1852, the library was removed to New Oxford-street, and year by year, as the business grew, house after house was added. These, with the great hall in their rear—one of the largest and best-proportioned rooms in London—hardly suffice to contain the vast accumulation of books which has been provided for the instruction and amusement of the multitude.

At the commencement of his enterprise, Mr. Mudie did not contemplate the circulation of works of fiction; but very soon afterwards it was quite clear to him that, as some of the best philosophy of the day came clothed in that attractive garb, it was not desirable to exclude them; and a considerable number of copies were taken of 'Margaret Maitland of Sunnyside,' 'Alton Locke,' 'Mary Barton,' 'Jane Eyre,' 'Vanity Fair,' and the earlier novels of the author of 'John Halifax;' and through the door, once open, a hundred other of the choicer novels found their way, and others followed—the difficulty of drawing any line, save for obvious reasons, having been frankly admitted.

It is almost a pity that the stricter rule and higher standard adopted in the first instance were not rigorously maintained throughout; but the principle of an index expurgatorius could never have commended itself to a man of Mr. Mudie's liberal views, and would never have been tolerated by the great multitude of his patrons.

Whether the library has accomplished all that might have been hoped for by the more sanguine of its early patrons, and whether, while offering the means of intellectual improvement and innocent enjoyment to many readers, it has not at the same time incidentally, and it may be injuriously, disturbed to some extent the old order of things, may be a matter of question; but as far as the founder is concerned, there can be no doubt that he has worked assiduously and effectually in the interests of literature.

Mr. Mudie is one of the members for Westminster of the London School Board; a director of the London Missionary Society; a Fellow of the Royal Geographical Society; and is, we believe, the author of a volume of poems called 'Stray Leaves,' of which some of the reviews speak in the highest terms.

LIONEL BROUGH.

Mr. Lionel Brough, the popular low comedian, is the son of the late Mr. Barnabas Brough, once well known as a dramatic author, writing under the nom de plume of 'Barnard de Burgh.'

Mr. Lionel Brough is a native of the Principality, having been born at Pontypool, in Monmouthshire, on March 10th, 1836. He is the brother of the late Robert and William Brough, known to all playgoers as the 'Brothers Brough,' and also of the late Mr. John C. Brough, author of works on scientific subjects, and the librarian to the London Institution.

Mr. Lionel Brough has taken to the stage; for, like many leading actors, he was not bred to the profession, but began life as clerk to Mr. John Timbs, editor of the 'Illustrated London News,' at the time when Douglas Jerrold, Albert Smith, John Leech, Charles Dickens, and W. M. Thackeray were in their prime; he was afterwards assistant publisher of the 'Daily Telegraph' for the first seven months of its existence.

He made his first appearance on the London stage at the Lyceum, under the celebrated management of Madame Vestris and Charles Mathews. The piece was an extravaganza entitled 'Prince Prettypet,' produced in December 1854. Madame Vestris died, and Mr. Mathews retired from the management of the Lyceum.

In 1858, Mr. Brough was again at the Lyceum under Mr. E. Falconer's management. He then deserted the stage, and was for five years on the 'Morning Star.' He next gave entertainments—'Cinderella,' 'Der Freischutz,' &c.—at the Polytechnic, afterwards travelling in the provinces with a 'Ghost' performance, which he produced 'by command' at Windsor. Mr. Brough played before the Queen and the late Prince Consort, with the members of the Savage Club, for the Lancashire Relief Fund, and also visited Liverpool and Manchester for the same object.

He next joined Mr. Henderson at the Prince of Wales's Theatre, Liver-

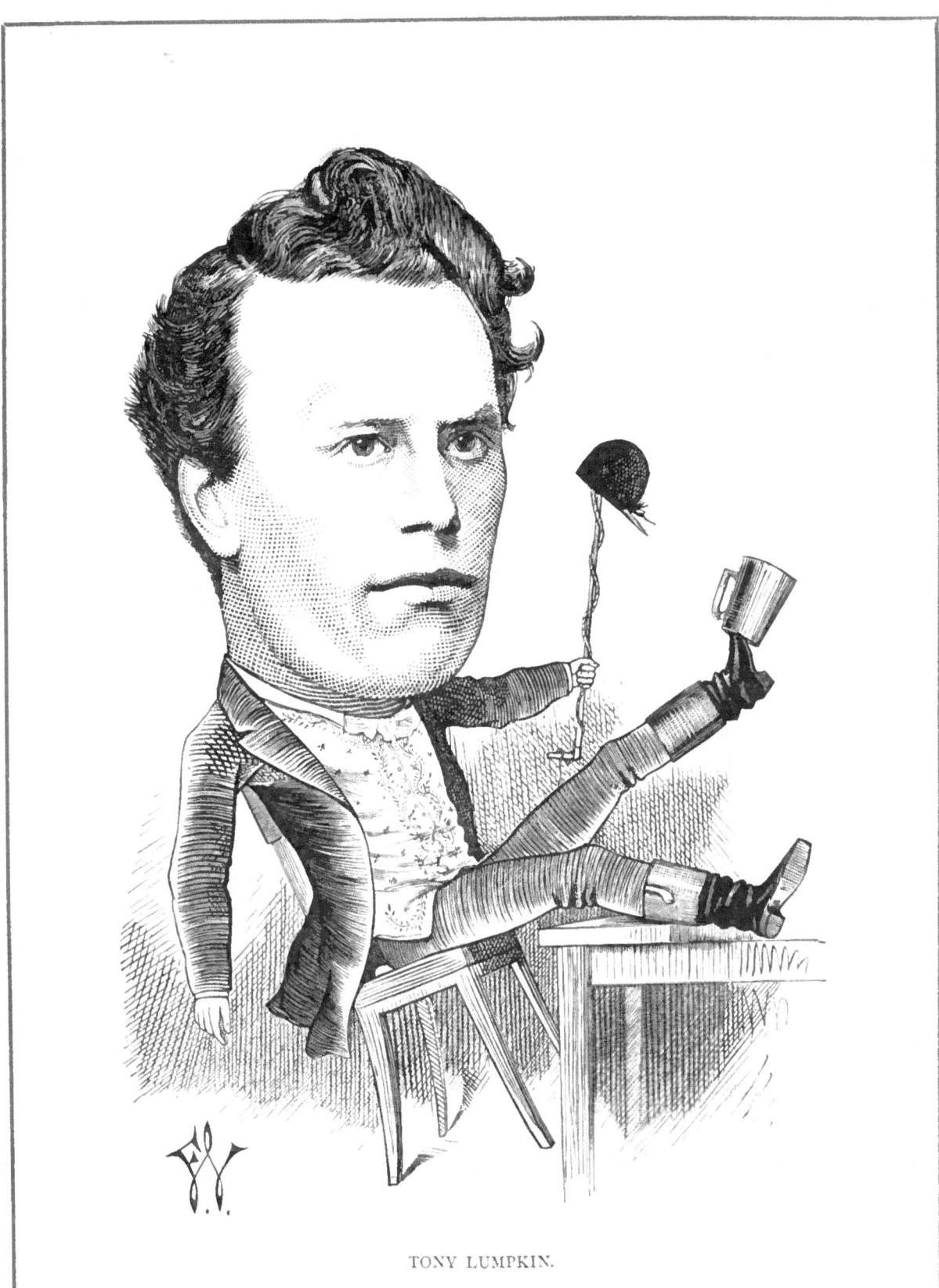

TONY LUMPKIN.

pool, afterwards becoming a member of Mr. Copeland's company at the Amphitheatre; and next was associated with Mr. Saker at the Alexandra Theatre there.

Mr. Brough came to London in October 1867, and has played at the Queen's, St. James's, and Holborn theatres. In August 1872, Mr. Boucicault opened Covent Garden—at the close of the Opera season—with Mr. Brough as his stage manager.

At Liverpool, Birmingham, Leeds, and the chief provincial towns, Mr. Brough has often performed, and is a great favourite with his audiences. He has all the requisite qualities as an actor for the parts he plays; and to his great natural humour and fun he adds a conscientious and careful study of the characters he undertakes.

Tony Lumpkin, in 'She Stoops to Conquer,' he played for a long time, with the greatest success, at the St. James's Theatre; and he is the best Tony on the stage. Uncle Ben in 'Dearer than Life,' Spotty in 'The Lancashire Lass,' Sampson Burr in 'The Porter's Knot,' Mark Meddle in 'London Assurance,' Robin Wildbriar in 'Extremes,' are among the best of Mr. Brough's assumptions. He plays them with marked intelligence and appreciation, and a display of genuine humorous power and versatility not too frequently met with on the stage.

Mr. Brough likewise enjoys considerable celebrity as an actor of burlesque parts, when he never fails to put his audiences in a good temper with themselves and with their entertainer.

WILKIE COLLINS.

The subject of our cartoon, Mr. Wilkie Collins, is one of the most successful novel writers of the day.

He is the eldest son of the late Mr. W. Collins, R.A., an artist of great ability in the delineation of rustic landscapes. Mr. Wilkie Collins was born in London in the year 1824, and received his education at a private school. He was associated with the late Charles Dickens in the celebrated amateur performances at Tavistock House. In 1859-60, his famous story of 'The Woman in White' appeared in 'All the Year Round.'

Besides 'The Woman in White,' Mr. Collins is the author of the following works of fiction: 'The Queen of Hearts,' 'No Name,' 'The Moonstone,' 'My Miscellanies,' 'Mr. Wray's Cash Box; or the Mask and the Mystery: a Christmas Sketch,' 'Man and Wife,' 'Poor Miss Finch', 'Miss or Mrs.,' 'Hide and Seek,' 'The Dead Secret,' 'Basil: a Story of Modern Life,' 'Armadale,' 'Antonina; or the Fall of Rome,' 'After Dark;' and he was, jointly with Charles Dickens, the author of two of the Christmas stories published as supplementary numbers of 'All the Year Round.'

He has written also a life of his father, Mr. W. Collins, R.A., published in 1848, entitled 'Memoirs of the Life of William Collins, with Selections from his Journal and Correspondence;' and a book of sketches called 'Rambles beyond Railways; or Notes in Cornwall taken a-Foot.'

As a writer of fiction, Mr. Collins is remarkable for the ingenuity of his plots, and for the air of mystery that he contrives to throw over commonplace events. He—in striking contrast to many writers of much greater eminence and merit—devotes the utmost care to keeping his story 'close together.' Everything in his books has a bearing on the issue of the plot. Not a window is opened, a door shut, or a nose blown, but, depend upon it, the act will have something to do with the end of the book. Yet no book of Mr. Collins's can compare in this respect with Scott's 'Bride of Lammer-

HE WROTE THE 'WOMAN IN WHITE.'

moor,' where every chapter is necessary—not one is redundant; where every line contributes to the final and splendidly effective climax. And in this quality alone can Mr. Collins's novels be compared, with advantage to their author, with the greater works of greater men.

His plots are commonly intricate. Often it is too difficult for the reader to hold all the threads for it to be a pleasant task to peruse his books, for he has the trick of ending every chapter with a bang. He is admirably suited to supply the wants of periodicals to whose readers a sensational story is the one attraction, *e. g.*

On the white dress of the child was traced, in letters of blood, the word 'HELP!'

This habit is contrary to every true principle of art, and is dictated, probably, by the wants of periodical literature.

The characters in Mr. Collins's books are some of them very original and striking, being manifestly sketches from real life; but the situations in which these puppets are placed by the wire-puller are often wildly improbable. 'Fact is stranger than fiction,' Mr. Collins will reply. Indeed, he threatens us with a production which shall put the plot of 'The Woman in White' in the shade, made from materials kindly sent him by various correspondents. These are, of course, narratives of fact.

His English is not drawn from the purest fount, nor is his literary style to be compared with that of several living writers. He is a manufacturer of interesting works of fiction, pure and simple. He has made it his business in life. And, under the circumstances, it is perhaps a little provoking that he should so often ring the changes on such phrases as 'my art,' 'my purpose in writing the book,' 'the object I had in view,' &c., as each of his later novels has probably brought him 4000*l*.

We should place 'Man and Wife' among his best productions; but in literature he will be remembered as the author of 'The Woman in White.' That wonderful story made him famous.

ALFRED TENNYSON.

It is about forty-two years since Mr. Tennyson issued his first volumes of poems. The young poet attracted little attention at the time, save from the critics, who could not understand 'this young man from Lincolnshire,' and so did the next best thing—namely, abused his verses. In 1833, Tennyson, nothing daunted, made his second appearance, only to be abused again, but this time in a quarter where virulent condemnation was—in that day at least—generally accepted by a new author as the best testimonial to his true merit. The 'Quarterly,' having killed Keats—or, at all events, having gained the reputation for doing it—was ready, like the ogres of the old fables, to annihilate any new victim. Mr. Tennyson, in his earlier poems more evidently than in his more mature efforts, had drawn much of his turn of thought and imagination from the author of 'Endymion.' With a charming expression, therefore, of contrition for its former bad treatment of 'the harbinger of the milky way of poetry'—as, even in its jesuitical apology, the 'Quarterly' still chose to designate Keats—it pointed its quill for the demolition of the later aspirant to poetic fame; with what ultimate success, the strong hold which Tennyson's writings have since taken on the affections of the reading portion of his countrymen is sufficiently palpable. But it is useful sometimes, if only for the benefit of poets yet unfledged, to point back to the rough handling which men who have now made their names encountered at the outset of their careers. And we do not know whether these very men, now reposing in the calm Hesperides of their success, are not inwardly thankful for the rough lessons which they received in the earlier days of their pilgrimage to fame. Faults and flaws have been pointed out, which the man of true genius has acknowledged to himself as the ordinary results of inexperience, and has accordingly rectified to the best of his power.

In Tennyson's earlier poems, for instance, there was an air of affectation

POET LAUREATE.

which, though pretty enough in its way, and a novel characteristic to a certain extent, yet betrayed a latent weakness. The same quality attaches to the Laureate's productions even now, to a limited extent. In fact, we doubt whether Tennyson could altogether get rid of the old trick; but his youthful effusions were overladen to a degree with these affectations.

The critic of the 'Quarterly' took good care to seize the weak points of the young Lincolnshire poet, and went mercilessly to work.

If only as amusing pictures of the old style of criticism, which in this more polite age has rarely been seen—except a few years ago in the coarse but vigorous criticisms of the 'Saturday Review,' when that journal possessed a power in the world of letters it has since lost by the death or secession of the men who made it famous—we may be excused for giving a few specimens of the reviewer's manner.

The poet has sung:

> Then let wise Nature work her will,
> And on my clay her darnels grow;
> Come only when the days are still,
> And at my headstone whisper low,
> And tell me—

'Now, what,' says the critic of the 'Quarterly,' 'would an ordinary bard wish to be told under such circumstances? Why, perhaps how his sweetheart was, or his child, or his family, or how the Reform Bill worked, or whether the last edition of the poems had been sold;—papæ! our genuine poet's first wish is:

> And tell me if the woodbines blow.

When, indeed, he shall have been thus satisfied as to the woodbines—of the blowing of which, in their due season, he may, we think, feel pretty secure—he turns a passing thought to his friend, and another to his mother.

> If thou art blest—my mother's smile
> Undimm'd—

But such inquiries, short as they are, seem too commonplace; and he immediately glides back into his curiosity as to the state of the forwardness of the spring.

> If thou art blest—my mother's smile
> Undimm'd—if bees are on the wing.

No, we believe the whole circle of poetry does not furnish such another instance of enthusiasm for the sights and sounds of the vernal season! The sorrows of a bereaved mother rank after the blossoms of the woodbine, and just before the hummings of the bee; and this is all he has any curiosity about, for he proceeds:

> Then cease, my friend, a little while,
> That I may—

"send my love to my mother;" or "give you some hints about bees, which I have picked up from Aristæus in the Elysian Fields;" or "tell you how I am situated as to my own personal comforts in the world below"? O, no!

> That I may hear the throstle sing
> His bridal song—the boast of spring.'

This is tolerably severe. The following lines, however, gave too palpable an opportunity for even the most obtuse critic to let slip:

> Sweet as the noise in parchèd plains
> Of bubbling wells that fret the stones
> (If any sense in me remains)
> Thy words will be, thy cheerful tones
> As welcome to—my crumbling bones.

And this is the commentary,

> 'If any sense in me remains!

This doubt is inconsistent with the opening stanza of the piece, and, in fact, too modest. We take upon ourselves to reassure Mr. Tennyson, that, even after he shall be dead and buried, as much "sense" will still remain as he has now the good fortune to possess.'

Take the following again:

'The accumulation of tender images in the following lines appears not less wonderful:

>   Remember you that pleasant day
>   When, after roving in the woods—
>   'Twas April then—I came and lay
>   Beneath those gummy chestnut buds?
>   A water-rat from off the bank
>   Plunged in the stream.   With idle care,
>   Down looking through the sedges rank,
>   I saw your troubled image there.
>   If you remember, you had set
>   Upon the narrow casement-edge
>   A long green box of mignonette,
>   And you were leaning on the ledge.

The poet's truth to nature in his "gummy chestnut buds," and to art in the "long green box" of mignonette, and that masterly touch of likening the first intrusion of love into the virgin bosom of the miller's daughter to the plunging of a water-rat into the mill-dam—these are beauties which, we do not fear to say, equal anything even in Keats.'

The most ardent admirers of Tennyson's earlier poems must confess that, in instances such as these, the poet laid himself open to the ridicule of an ill-natured reviewer.

One more example of this, and we have done with the Laureate's more youthful efforts. In the 'Dream of Fair Women,' we all know the exquisite description of Iphigenia, and have most of us noted that flaw in the closing lines,

>   The tall masts quiver'd as they lay afloat;
>   The temples, and the people, and the shore;
>   One drew a sharp knife through my tender throat,
>   Slowly, and nothing more.

The critic's chance here is of course inevitable.

'What touching simplicity! What pathetic resignation! "He cut my throat—*nothing more!*" One might ask, "What more she would have?"'

The line has been altered in the later editions of the poet's works; but we have merely recalled some of these earlier defects of the Laureate's muse to show that even great poets—though born, not made—must always owe much to long and elaborate culture, and must pass through the crucible in repeated refinings before their works are fit to remain the last polished evidences to posterity of their innate genius.

Upon this principle, Tennyson is undoubtedly the most polished poet of modern times; but it is a question whether, in his extreme cultivation, he has not sacrificed much of that manly vigour which some of his contemporaries — Browning and Swinburne, for instance — have displayed in their works, either with an unpopular abruptness, or, in the case of the latter poet at times, with a still more unpopular license. Yet Tennyson, with all his weaknesses, is Laureate of the day, as much by a pretty generally recognised right of sovereignty as by title. He has written much that is deliciously sweet—much that is grandly chivalrous. His ear for the music of our fine old Saxon language is perfect. He is almost always intelligible; and, above all, he has never written a word to raise a blush even on the most modest cheek. He is a worthy successor of Wordsworth in the laureateship; and although we have had greater poets even in this nineteenth century, and may yet see greater than those at present in the field before its close, Alfred Tennyson may well claim the first place among living bards.

Indiscriminate praise, which popularity for the time being naturally induces, is always damaging to an author's permanent reputation. For this reason, at the risk of not being seconded in our opinions by the more enthusiastic admirers of the Laureate, let us consider briefly the salient characteristics of Tennyson's writings.

In the first place, except at occasional intervals, his poetry has been essentially objective rather than subjective. A lover of external things of beauty, a student of nature rather than of men, a dreamer rather than a man of action, he—like his own 'Lotus Eaters'—yields rather to the seductive influence of sensuous attractions than to the impulse of more restless minds, who would fain step forth, and, taking the living world for their theme, suggest with prophetic voice the lessons which depend upon the present for the benefit of the unborn future. With rare instances has he touched upon the crying needs of the day—upon the problems which our growing civilisation all over the world is ever presenting. Calm, pensive, retrospective, he is most at his ease when drawing for the fountains of his inspiration from the mellow fancies of the old classical mythology or Arthurian legends.

It may be objected that such poems as 'Locksley Hall' and 'Lady Clara Vere de Vere' are contradictions to this theory; but it must be remembered that these, after all, are but random wanderings from the main path which the Laureate first marked out for himself, and has, in the main, persistently trodden since.

In his earlier poems we find him revelling in the old Homeric traditions, around which he has thrown the magic of a charm peculiarly his own. In these poems we hear, in that exquisite fragment, 'Morte d'Arthur,' the first tentative notes of the song which was later on to burst into the wondrous and sustained melody of his masterpiece, the 'Idylls of the King.' And on this poem, above all others, we think Tennyson's reputation must rest with later generations. Almost Homeric in its breadth and simplicity, it combines the homely pathos, the picturesque variety, and the teeming allegory of our elder minstrels, with the polished grace which springs from a complete command of the highest resources of modern art. The exquisite blank verse—of which, perhaps, no greater master than Tennyson can be named—flows on with an utter disguise of all elaboration and effort. Art has concealed the traces of art. There is no perceptible straining after effect, no struggling to elaborate startling points. The narrative is told with exquisite grace and beauty; and some of the charming lyrics which form the interludes have a delicious cadence which haunts the memory like a melody of Mendelssohn's.

In the 'Idylls of the King' we see Tennyson's characteristic merits at their highest. In it he has taken a field for himself, in which all imitators —and they have been many, no less a poet than Lord Lytton among the number—have signally failed; and here at least, in his capacity of throwing a radiance of new life and beauty about the mouldering legends of antiquity, the Laureate has proved himself unrivalled by living bards.

To compare him with, or to gauge him by, the standard of any of his famous predecessors, as has been sometimes done, would be idle. Like all great artists, he has learnt and adapted from the finest models before him. Beyond this, he is a poet per se, and this is his greatest praise.

Mr. Tennyson was born in 1810 at the parsonage of Somerby, a quiet hamlet in the neighbourhood of Spilsby, in Lincolnshire. Somerby and

Enderby form a rectory once held by the poet's father, the Rev. George Clayton Tennyson, D.D., the eldest brother of Mr. Tennyson D'Eyncourt, who was for some years member of Parliament for one of the metropolitan boroughs. As a boy, the future Poet Laureate was sent to the grammar-school of Louth, and afterwards proceeded to Trinity College, Cambridge—Thackeray being at the University at the same time. In 1829 he gained the Chancellor's medal for the best English poem, the subject for the year being 'Timbuctoo.'

After leaving Cambridge, he spent much of his time in travelling about from place to place, from London to Hastings, Hastings to Cheltenham, to Eastbourne, to Twickenham—everywhere, in fact, where he might find food for that love of the beautiful in nature so characteristic of his poems. His first productions, as we have already said, attracted little public notice; but when people became awake to the nervous passion of 'Locksley Hall,' the indignant satire of 'Lady Clara Vere de Vere,' the tender beauty of 'The May Queen,' and the sensuous elegance of such poems as 'A Dream of Fair Women,' 'The Sleeping Beauty,' and 'The Palace of Art,' his claim as a poet of a high order was universally admitted.

How emphatically he has strengthened and enlarged his reputation by those later and more ambitious works with which we are all familiar, needs no remark.

On the death of Wordsworth, Mr. Tennyson was, it is generally understood at the express desire of the Queen, in 1851 appointed Poet Laureate; and he received at the same time, from Sir Robert Peel, the grant of a pension of 200*l.* per annum.

From this time he began to produce those works with which his fame is more eminently associated. For twenty years he has been Laureate; and during that period we have had at intervals—for Tennyson is by no means a prolific author—'Maud,' which appeared in 1855; the 'Idylls of the King,' in 1858; 'Enoch Arden,' in 1864; 'The Holy Grail,' in 1869; and 'Gareth and Lynette' in 1872. Besides these, he has contributed occasional poems to the magazines, the most notable among these being 'Tithonus,' which first appeared in the 'Cornhill Magazine;' and the fine philosophic study entitled 'Lucretius,' in 'Macmillan.'

NORMAN MACLEOD, D.D.

The late Rev. Norman Macleod, D.D., one of her Majesty's chaplains for Scotland, was born in 1812. His father, of the same name as himself, was in his time a distinguished minister of the Church of Scotland, in which the son held such a prominent place.

Dr. Macleod was educated at the Universities of Edinburgh and Glasgow; and, after holding various minor preferments in the Established Church of Scotland, was appointed minister of the Barony Church in Glasgow.

He was known as the author of many valuable and interesting works; and perhaps the most noticeable, his book entitled 'Eastward,' based upon his experiences of travels which he made in Palestine and the neighbouring countries some years ago, added largely to his reputation as an attractive writer. Dr. Macleod also went, in 1867, on a journey of inspection among the principal missionary stations of India—a thousand pounds having been previously voted to him for travelling expenses from the funds devoted to missionary enterprises by the Established Church of Scotland.

Some of the more interesting results of his investigations were given in 'Good Words,' of which Dr. Macleod was the editor from the first establishment of that magazine in the year 1860 to his death. These notes have since been reprinted in a volume form, under the title of 'Peeps at the Far East; or a Familiar Account of a Visit to India.'

Of his other numerous literary works, we may mention the 'Home School; or Hints on Home Education,' 'Simple Truths spoken to Working Men'—addressed more immediately to the congregation of the working classes of the Barony Mission Chapel—'Deborah,' 'Reminiscences of a Highland Parish,' and, perhaps one of the most successful of all his works, 'The Earnest Student.' Although only a brief sketch, one of the most character-

ONE OF HER MAJESTY'S CHAPLAINS.

istic examples of his style of thought and expression is a short disquisition on 'Social Life in Heaven'—one of the papers in a collection entitled 'Recognition of Friends in Heaven,' the joint production of the Bishop of Ripon, Dr. Macleod, J. B. Owen, M.A., and three other authors. Dr. Macleod wrote also an interesting Scottish story, 'The Starling.

ANDREW HALLIDAY.

Mr. ANDREW HALLIDAY DUFF—so well known in connection with literature and the drama as Mr. Andrew Halliday—is the son of the Rev. William Duff, of Grange, Banffshire, whose family is derived from Macduff, thane of Fife. He was born in 1830, and was educated at the Marischal College and University of Aberdeen, where he applied himself to the study of the classics, under Professor John Stuart Blackie.

Mr. Halliday began his literary career in London as a contributor to the 'Morning Chronicle,' and afterwards joined the 'Leader,' also contributing largely to various newspapers in London and the provinces. He next turned his attention to the stage; and in 1858, in conjunction with Mr. Lawrence, wrote the burlesque of 'Kenilworth,' which achieved a remarkable success at the Strand Theatre, and has held the stage ever since, having been constantly revived in London and the provinces. Mr. Halliday produced two other burlesques, one founded on 'Romeo and Juliet,' brought out at the Strand, the other on the subject of 'The Lady of the Lake,' and entitled 'Mountain Dhu,' at the Adelphi. In conjunction with the late Mr. William Brough, he wrote a great number of original farces, which were produced at the Adelphi, Drury-lane, the Lyceum, and other theatres. The principal of these were 'The Census,' 'The Pretty Horsebreaker,' 'A Valentine,' 'A Shilling Day at the Exhibition,' 'The Area Belle,' 'Doing Banting,' 'The Actor's Retreat,' 'My Heart's in the Highlands,' 'An April Fool,' 'Going to the Dogs,' 'The Mudborough Election,' 'The Colleen Bawn Married and Settled,' and a petite drama entitled 'The Wooden-Spoon Maker.'

In 1861, Mr. Halliday joined Charles Dickens's staff on 'All the Year Round,' and contributed regularly to that periodical until Mr. Dickens's death. He wrote at the same time for the 'Cornhill' and other magazines. Mr. Halliday's collected essays were published in three separate volumes, respectively entitled 'Everyday Papers,' 'Sunnyside Papers,' and 'Town

A SUCCESSFUL DRAMATIST.

and Country.' The 'Everyday Papers' went through several editions, and enjoyed a remarkable success. The 'Examiner,' criticising these essays, said:

'Mr. Halliday has a lively wit, with a soul to it in his quick wholesome feeling. He writes with a light touch, but without frivolity; his gaiety is intellectual, his English accurate. His papers, light and refreshing, supply already to our current literature some of the best of the reading that seeks chiefly to amuse. We are convinced that they are the earnest of better things to come.'

A criticism by no means too favourable.

In 1867, Mr. Halliday produced his first important dramatic work, 'The Great City,' at Drury-lane. It was brought out on Easter Monday. The piece had—at Drury-lane—the unprecedented run of a hundred nights. 'King o' Scots,' 'Amy Robsart,' and 'Rebecca' followed, each piece carrying the manager triumphantly through the entire season, without the necessity for change. In 1869, he produced 'Little Em'ly,' an adaptation of 'David Copperfield'—with the sanction of Mr. Dickens—which ran two hundred nights at the Olympic Theatre. 'Nell,' an adaptation of 'The Old Curiosity Shop,' followed at the same house. 'Notre Dame' was produced at the Adelphi on Easter Monday 1871. The piece had a run of two hundred and fifty-six nights.

Mr. Halliday was the editor of the 'Savage-Club Papers,' very popular among a large class of readers.

Mr. Chatterton said, at Drury-lane, 'Byron spelt bankruptcy and Shakspeare ruin' for him as a manager. With Mr. Halliday's assistance, he has had some of the greatest successes ever known at Drury-lane.

CANON KINGSLEY.

The Reverend Charles Kingsley, M.A., rector of Eversley, canon of Chester, one of her Majesty's chaplains, tutor to the Prince of Wales, and Professor of Modern History in the University of Cambridge, was born on the 12th of June 1819 at Holme Vicarage, on the borders of Dartmoor. He became at fourteen a pupil of the Rev. Derwent Coleridge—son of Samuel Taylor Coleridge—and afterwards was a student at King's College, London. He then entered at Magdalen College, Cambridge, where he was a scholar and prizeman whilst in statu pupillari, and concluded his undergraduate career with a good degree—first class in classics, and second class in mathematics.

Mr. Kingsley entered the Church; and his first cure was the rectory he now holds; for a year and a half after his entering upon his curacy the living became vacant, and the patron, Sir John Cope, presented it to the curate, who has ever since been rector of Eversley.

Charles Kingsley's name, however, was to be known and honoured, far away from his little Hampshire parish, as the writer of works of fiction which are strikingly original, pure in their moral teaching, honest and noble in their purpose, and have placed their author high in the ranks of writers of imaginative literature.

The list of Mr. Kingsley's works includes 'Westward Ho! or the Voyages and Adventures of Sir Amyas Leigh,' now in a sixth edition; a splendid story, photographing for the reader the grand scenery of the newly found continent of America, and exhibiting the adventurous and noble spirit of the age in which the scenes of Sir Amyas Leigh's adventures are laid.

'Two Years Ago,' and the author's latest book, 'At Last: a Christmas in the West Indies,' contain likewise much of that word-painting, applied to the description of natural scenery, in which Charles Kingsley is a master.

'Hypatia; or New Foes with an Old Face,' is a most interesting story

MODERN HISTORY.

of an early state of society, in which the author has completely thrown himself back into the period he has written about, with such a power of artistic reality as to make his characters live again.

'Yeast: a Problem,' and 'Alton Locke,' are books that deal with social problems arising out of a high state of civilisation; and although now much in 'Alton Locke' belongs to a bygone generation, such characters as the Young Tailor-Poet and Old Sandy Mackaye will always charm and interest those who make their acquaintance.

'Water Babies' and 'The Heroes' are two books of fairy tales for children. Considering their object, they are admirable productions, and very much more acceptable to a child than such books as 'Lewis Carroll's' tales.

'Hereward the Wake, Last of the English,' is a story of the time of the Norman Conquest; a period of history with which the author is perfectly acquainted: it was the subject of some of his lectures at Cambridge, where he was the more popular of the two popular professors—Mr. Fawcett, M.P. for Brighton, was the other. His manner of delivering his addresses on history, from the high chair in the old cellar called the Arts School, was very piquant. He is reported to have summed up a great event in English history thus: 'Gentlemen, believe me, if Edward the Confessor had only had the common decency to get married, there would have been no Norman Conquest in England.' We will not vouch for the verbal accuracy of the sentence, but the learned professor said something to the same effect. The undergraduates used to cheer him, and strangers in Cambridge always went to hear him lecture. He was never dry, often he was eloquent; but he had an odd way of ending his bursts with a sentence something like that given above.

He was popular in the University; at his own college he was beloved. When he was the only Don to go in to the high table, and a few minutes late, and, according to custom, the undergraduates were waiting for a Don to say grace before they could begin, contemplating with impatience the cooling dishes, the Professor of History, who knows the British nature well, would instruct the butler to 'Tell those poor boys not to wait for me: let them begin their dinner.'

It is curious to note that the critics were very severe with Kingsley and

F. D. Maurice about the same time and for the same reasons—under the disguise of Christian Socialism they would level everything into nothingness, if they could. They have triumphed, and their names are honoured above those of most men of their generation. No writers of our time have done more for truth and manliness, or sown seed more likely to bear fruit in its season. It was in 1859 that Charles Kingsley was appointed to his Cambridge professorship, and we owe at least two of his best works to his study of what, at that University, is called 'Modern History.'

GEORGE AUGUSTUS SALA.

Mr. George Augustus Sala was born in London about the year 1826. He is the son of a Portuguese gentleman, who married an English lady. Having adopted literature as his profession, Mr. Sala became a writer in 'Household Words,' which was edited by the late Charles Dickens. He also contributed to the 'Illustrated London News,' 'Cornhill Magazine,' and other papers and periodicals, until, in 1863, he went out to the United States as special correspondent for the 'Daily Telegraph.' On his return, he published his observations under the title of 'My Diary in America in the Midst of War.'

He also wrote a series of very graphic letters for the 'Daily Telegraph' from Algeria, during the Emperor's visit to that colony.

The following is a list of Mr. Sala's best-known works : 'A Journey due North: a Residence in Russia,' 1856; 'How I tamed Mrs. Cruiser,' 1858; 'Twice Round the Clock,' 1859; 'Gaslight and Daylight,' 1859; 'The Baddington Peerage,' 1860; 'Lady Chesterfield's Letters to her Daughter,' 1860; 'William Hogarth,' 1860; 'Looking at Life,' 1860; 'Make your Game,' 1860; 'Dutch Pictures,' 1861; 'Accepted Addresses,' 1862; 'Breakfast in Bed,' 1863; 'After Breakfast;' 'The Perfidy of Captain Slyboots,' 1863; 'Quite Alone' (finished by another writer), 1864; 'Robson: a Sketch,' 1864; 'Seven Sons of Mammon,' 1864; 'My Diary in America in the Midst of War,' 1865; 'From Waterloo to the Peninsula,' 1866; 'A Trip to Barbary by a Roundabout Route,' 1866; 'The Strange Adventures of Captain Dangerous,' 1869; 'The Two Prima Donnas,' 1869; 'Rome and Venice,' 1869.

'Gaslight and Daylight' is composed of short papers of very great humour and merit. 'Papers Humorous and Pathetic' contains 'The Key of the Street,' 'Colonel Quagg's Conversion,' and other sketches, arranged by the author in a form suitable for public reading. Better papers for plat-

A SPECIAL CORRESPONDENT.

CHARLES LEVER.

Born August 31, 1809; died June 1, 1872.

Two worlds there are in which we live and move—
    The world of fiction and the world of fact:
One of King Magic, whom his subjects love;
    One of King Fate, wherein we talk and act.

In one, the good men fail, the bad succeed;
    Age carves its lines too soon on buxom youth:
Man falls ignobly in the hour of need,
    And woman's faith beats down our faith in truth.

Here sickness weakens; here high purpose dies;
    Here lofty aims are kill'd; here few are brave;
Here, torn by vultures, great Prometheus lies;
    Here hope is crush'd, work bounded by the grave.

But there, O great magicians! there we dwell,
    Robed in forgetfulness of present woe,
Languid and still, on beds of asphodel,
    While the unheeded hours pass by and go.

There beauty fades not, smiles change not to tears,
    Mirth never palls, and wine doth not destroy;
Love is immortal, manhood has no fears;
    No cloud is there 'tween sunshine and our joy.

O world of fiction!—all unreal, yet true—
    What fit thanks can we frame our debt to meet?
And for thy chiefs what crown of praise is due,
    If any crown is dear to them we greet?

The kings and statesmen pass across the stage—
    They vex the world and us—and then they die:
Forgotten soon, save where on history's page
    Dry lists of dead men's names make schoolboys sigh.

THYSELF IN THY LIKENESS. *Tempest*, act iii. sc. 2.

But these, our writers—when one dies, the hours
    Are hush'd awhile, because they could not save;
And smiles and tears, like sunshine cross'd by flowers,
    Arch an eternal rainbow o'er his grave.

Never forgotten—yet we mourn his loss,
    As of some friend long loved and deeply tried;
Or as of sunshine that has lain across
    So long, we eem d it ne'er would leave our side.

Therefore, when tidings came, how in fair spring
    Death had seized one whose heart no winter knew,
Great sadness fell on us, remembering
    Days of our youth, when things seem'd fair and true;

When we lay, deep beneath the apple shade,
    In an old orchard all the afternoon;
Above us, pink and white, the blossoms spread;
    Flowers at our feet, and all around us June.

And then we read the tales of war and Spain;
    Of revelry and Ireland, sword and gown;
Of love that mock'd at bars put up in vain;
    Of hardihood that trampled danger down;

Proctors and doctors, undergrads, dragoons,
    Vivandières, and priests, and muleteers gay;
Groves dear to maidens, soldiers, stars, and moons,
    Swept past our fancy in their wild array.

And is he dead, who told so well—whose pen
    Grew wise, but never dull—whose laughter rang,
If not so loud, as genial still as when
    Among his Dublin monks he drank and sang?

Farewell, Charles Lever! Could fate overlook,
    But for one other work, thy fruitful days.
Farewell! the world is gloomier. Ill we brook
    To lose thy voice in Joy's small choir of Praise.

Charles James Lever, the writer of so many brilliant works of fiction, was born in Dublin, in the year 1809. He was educated there at Trinity College, and was originally intended to follow the medical profession; but he soon abandoned physic for literature, and so followed the bent of his great natural genius. From 'Harry Lorrequer,' completed about the year 1836, to 'Lord Kilgobbin,' only recently finished in 'The Cornhill,' Charles Lever wrote a very large number of works of fiction of great merit. His wise and witty essays in 'Blackwood,' under the nom de plume of Cornelius O'Dowd, have been universally admired, as have his numerous contributions to 'All the Year Round,' 'St. Pauls,' and the columns of 'Once a Week.' The proximate cause of his death—which took place at Trieste, on the 1st of June 1872—was disease of the heart. This sad event was expected by his relatives and friends, and calmly contemplated by himself. His letters of late were full of allusions to the shattered state of his health, and he often mentioned his belief that he had not long to live. Still his brightness and fun never left him, and he was the good, genial, and amiable Charles Lever to the last days of his life; and every reader of his writings will cordially echo the words of a writer in 'Blackwood,' that 'we have lost in Charles Lever one of those brilliant and cheering lights the extinction of which may be said to "eclipse the gaiety of nations."'

J. R. PLANCHÉ.

A very interesting and amusing book, entitled 'The Recollections and Reflections of J. R. Planché (Somerset Herald),' has recently been given to the world.

Mr. Planché's grandfather was a French refugee, but his parents, both of French stock, were born in London. The author of the 'Recollections' made his first appearance on life's stage in Old Burlington-street, on the 27th of February 1796. He is therefore seventy-six years of age, and is as active in the prosecution of his literary pursuits as ever he was. Besides publishing this year the book above mentioned, he has furnished the stage with the lyrical parts of 'Babil and Bijou,' Mr. Boucicault's great show at Covent-garden. Mr. Planché's father was an eminent watchmaker, and attracted the notice of George III., who often chatted with him in the most familiar manner. He tells this characteristic anecdote of that monarch:

One day, going to St. James's with the king's watch, which had been mended, he told the page that the ribbon was rather dirty.

The king overheard this, and coming to the door, said:

'What is that, Planché? what is that?'

Mr. Planché repeated his remark about the state of the royal ribbon, and suggested a new one.

'New ribbon, Planché!' said the king. 'What for? Can't it be washed?'

This excellent gentleman, having known what it was to be very poor, determined that his son should learn some useful profession or trade. At first, the subject of our notice tried artistic pursuits, but having a very strong development of the cacoëthes scribendi, he chose to be articled to a bookseller. Soon after, he turned his attention to playwriting, and became distinguished as an amateur actor of his own characters. His early recollections date back to the destruction by fire of both the great national theatres; the Old-Prices row at new Covent-garden; the Young-Roscius mania; the

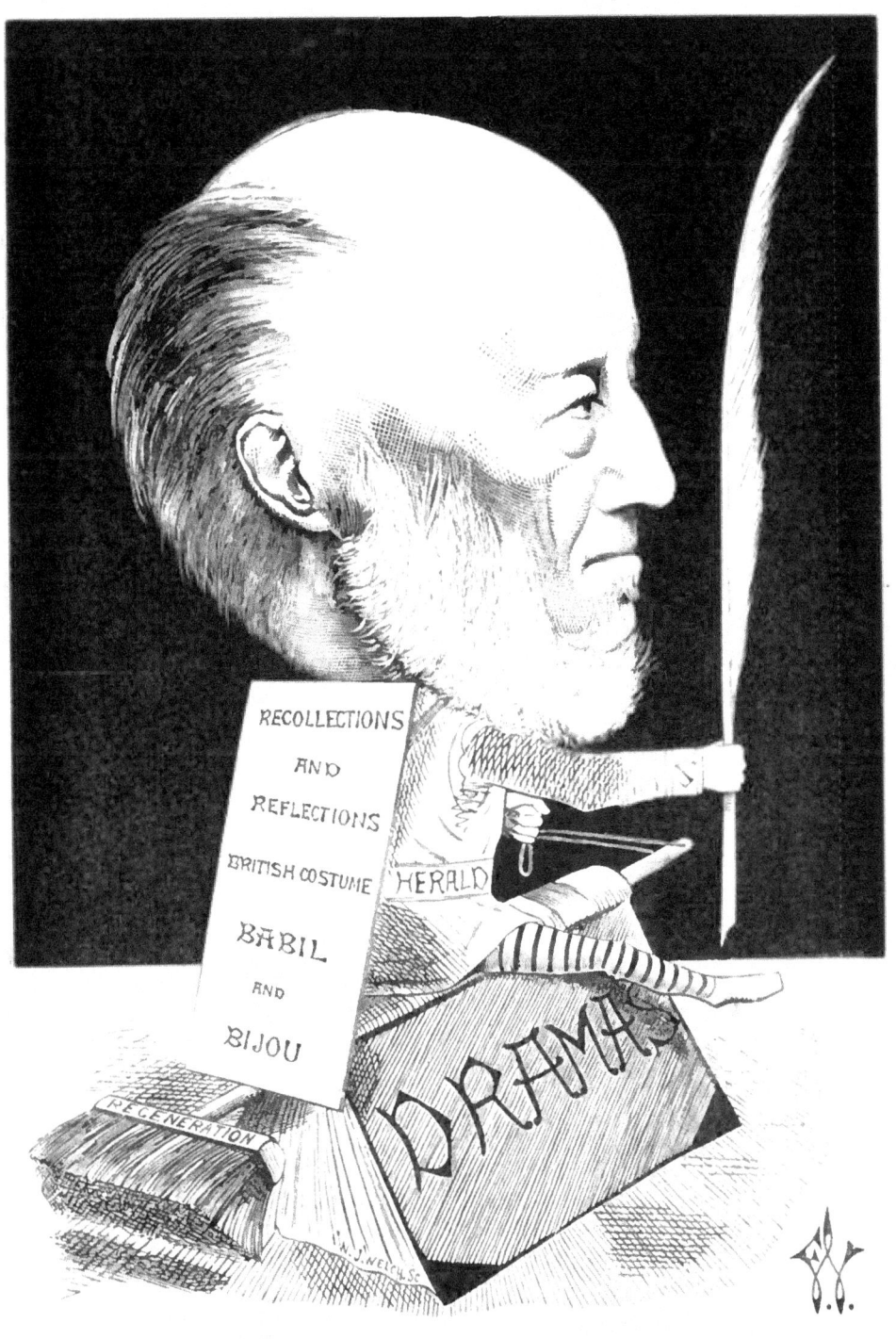

HERALD AND PLAYWRIGHT.

retirement of John Kemble and Mrs. Siddons; and the appearance of Edmund Kean and Miss O'Neil.

In 1818 'Amoroso,' a piece of his own, was produced at Drury-lane, and for fifty-four years Mr. Planché has been writing for the stage. In 1820 the 'Vampire' was brought out at the Lyceum.

It was three years after this that Mr. Planché began his reform of the costume of the stage: he designed the dresses for 'King John,' in accordance with the true dresses of the period, *gratuitously* for John Kemble. On the subject of costume, Mr. Planché is the greatest authority we have. It is a matter to which he has devoted many years of earnest study; and he may be regarded as the originator of correct dressing on the stage. This rehabilitation of the characters in 'King John' was thoroughly successful, and, he says, 'a complete reformation of dramatic costume became from that moment inevitable on the English stage.'

On the subject of old armour, too, Mr. Planché is a great authority; and he more than once arranged the splendid collection of the late Sir Samuel Meyrick for public exhibition.

While his own story of his life is by no means overburdened by reflections, it contains a fund of most interesting recollections. Without following the autobiographer year by year, we may say, in a few words, that it has been the fortune of the amiable and accomplished playwriter and antiquary to know intimately almost all the notabilities of the stage who have flourished from his youth to the present day; whilst in society he has been everywhere welcome, and has seen and known nearly everybody of social distinction; his office of Herald has brought him into immediate contact with kings and courts; and his descriptions of courtly scenes, at home and abroad, are not the least interesting portion of his memoirs.

EDMUND YATES.

MISSIONS to the United States have become quite the rage of late years; the passion for crossing the Atlantic seems to have seized a number of English literary men at about the same time, and probably for much the same reason. They had seen one or two very popular authors come back to their native land with pockets crammed with Yankee dollars, a result very desirable in itself; while the reports that reached England of the dinners, receptions, and galas given in honour of white elephants in the States filled these untravelled authors with delight. Added to all this, a sea voyage is said to have a fine effect in setting up constitutions enervated by a humdrum existence at home. Among these birds of passage one of the latest to wing his flight over the stormy ocean is Mr. Edmund Yates, an English novelist now on a tour, the object of which is to correct American misimpressions of the state of English institutions, society, and literature.

Mr. Yates is the son of the well-known actor, who was for a considerable period lessee of the old Adelphi Theatre. He was born in July 1831, and, like Mr. Anthony Trollope, has been connected with the Civil Service. Mr. Yates was for some time chief of the Missing-Letter Department in the Post Office. During his literary career he has been a constant contributor to periodical literature; and was for six years theatrical critic of the 'Daily News.' He was also at one time the editor of 'Temple Bar.' The articles signed 'The Flâneur,' in the late 'Morning Star,' were from his pen. His best novels are 'Broken to Harness,' 1864; 'Running the Gauntlet,' 1865; Black Sheep,' 1867; 'A Waiting Race,' and 'The Yellow Flag,' 1872.

A WAITING RACE.

CAPTAIN WARREN, R.E.

Captain Warren's name is so well known as associated with the recent excavations at Jerusalem as to need but little notice. These works were carried on in the teeth of the most formidable difficulties; against religious prejudices which had to be carefully 'managed,' against an unhealthy climate, against shortness in the finance department, and against great personal risks. We are not here going to recall the leading features of those explorations; suffice it to say that their results are of such great importance as to set the question of the holy sites upon an entirely different footing. Other travellers have preceded Captain Warren; none of them explored as he did, nor perhaps ever will again.

The shafts pierced through the rubbish were little holes, from three to four feet square. Their sides were walled up with wood, which was continually being 'started.' They were pierced to a depth sometimes of eighty, ninety, or even a hundred feet; galleries being run out from thence to examine along a wall, or to follow up a trace. Sometimes an aqueduct would be discovered, dry and empty, or foul with the tricklings of sewage overhead. Down this would crawl El Captan, as the Arabs called him, note-book in hand and pencil in mouth, measuring, sketching, and examining; for nothing must be left undescribed. Who could tell but that some lucky accident, some unexpected clue, might not lead at once to the solution of all the difficulties? Then the stuff through which the digging had to be conducted was so penetrated with the sewage of the town, that if the fingers were ever so slightly scratched, festering would ensue. And—which was the greatest anxiety of all—the lives of a hundred workmen and more, to say nothing of the gallant non-commissioned officers under his charge, were in the hands of Captain Warren. An error of judgment, a carelessly protected shaft, and all would be over in a moment. During all his work, he *never lost a man.*

JERUSALEM RECOVERED.

The account, chiefly an official statement, of his results was published originally in a connected form in 'The Recovery of Jerusalem.' The work was intended for students; and those who had not made what is called the Jerusalem question a serious study found it a dry and uninteresting work, lightened by the little bits of personal adventure. The Palestine Exploration Fund have issued a popular account of all their work, in continuous order, including the researches of the other officers who have worked for them. In this account full justice is done to the pluck, intelligence, and zeal of the gallant officer whose portrait we have given. Captain Warren, we have only to add, has found himself unable to go out again to the Holy Land; and has rejoined his corps, the Royal Engineers.

JOHN RUSKIN.

Mr. John Ruskin was born in London in 1819. He gained the Newdigate Prize for English verse at Oxford in 1839. Four years afterwards, in 1843, the first volume of his great work, 'Modern Painters,' appeared. The object with which the book was begun was a very noble one. It was to defend an old man and very great artist from the attacks of critics, who neither understood Turner's pictures nor his art. On its first appearance the book was rather scoffed at; but as it contained great truths about art, expressed in language of unsurpassed purity and eloquence, it soon made its way into circles beyond the reach of the critics. Three years afterwards, the second volume of 'Modern Painters' was published. Ten years after that, the third volume appeared; and it was not until 1860 that the book was completed.

Altogether, seventeen years elapsed between the first appearance of 'Modern Painters' and the completion of this great work.

It would be impossible in a small space to give a clear analysis of the contents of the five volumes of which it is composed. The motive for the publication of the first volume we have stated. This was the vindication of the greatest genius the English school of painters has produced from the calumnies of the then existing writers on art.

Turner was the butt of their ignorance. The only element necessary to the composition of a critic they seem to have possessed was an acquaintance with the art of penmanship. That generation has passed away; and we may thank Mr. Ruskin for having left the race of art-critics who have taken the place of the writers of 1843 no excuse for being ignorant of the elements or sources of pleasure in art—ideas of truth, of beauty, and of relation.

'In these books of mine,' says their author, 'their distinctive character as essays on art is their bringing everything to a root in a human passion or hope;' and he adds that they arose first, 'not in any desire to explain

ART CRITICISM.

the principles of art, but in the endeavour to defend an individual painter from injustice.'

In that endeavour, it is now almost superfluous to say, the book was entirely successful. The high prices that Turner's latest and less generally admired pictures brought in his own lifetime, and the magnificent sums that even drawings of a few inches square from his hand have been sold for since his death, prove the efficiency of Ruskin's advocacy.

He did 'defend an individual painter from injustice'—that painter the greatest of his age—with a penetration into the hidden truths of art; a critical insight invaluable and perhaps unique; a clearness of argument, a splendour of imaginative illustration, and an eloquence and purity of diction, which have hardly been surpassed by any English writer. No inconsiderable part of the estimation in which the works of the miserly and eccentric genius—a barber's son, who saw scarlet in the sky—are held to-day among the dilettanti is the result of Ruskin's criticism upon them.

The author of 'Modern Painters' is not only the first among English art-critics, but he is the first of them. Before his time, no writer on art of our country had a European reputation. The name of Reynolds was well known, it is true, in connection not only with his works as a painter, but with his 'Discourses' delivered when he was President of the Academy; but although these lectures contained much information gathered during a long and laborious study of art, they are, after all, but a text-book for students, and owe their modern reputation to the simple and chaste style in which they are written, and the excellent advice they give to young artists, rather than to any pretensions either to elevated criticism or masterly acquaintance with the whole of the wide subject on which they treat.

We once heard a bishop recommend their perusal to a number of young men whom he had ordained, as models for their sermons, on the ground that Sir Joshua's celebrated 'Discourses' contained 'very fine moral precepts, besides being written in very elegant English.'

This was true. Though the President's lectures had neither the fire of Burke, nor the wit and power of Johnson, they possessed great literary merit, and were as much above the art-writers of their day as Ruskin's 'Modern Painters' was above the criticism of 1843.

At the present day there are many competent writers on art topics who furnish the critiques on recent exhibitions to the papers and magazines; but a quarter of a century ago ignorance of the principles and practice of art seems to have been a passport to the post of art-critic.

On a most influential North-of-England paper, furnished for many years with independent reports on all matters of importance, this post of art-critic—being, as it was thought, easy and desirable—went by seniority: the oldest reporter got it. And we well remember hearing an anecdote of a respectable parliamentary reporter of the paper to whom the post of art and theatrical critic was offered. He accepted it as a matter of course. Being conscientious, he thought a little knowledge necessary, and asked a friend a few days after, 'What does' (naming a great musician) 'charge a lesson, do you know?' 'Good dear me, F——, why, at your time of life, you are never going to learn the fiddle!' 'No,' was the reply; 'but I've got to do the music and so on for the "—— Guardian," and I mean to take two or three lessons, for I know no more of music than a cow.'

We believe that the London papers of thirty or forty years ago were dealt with in much the same way; and a number of intelligent and honest gentlemen, who knew no more of painting than a cow, 'did' the criticisms. And nothing is easier than to parade the jargon of art language—to talk of light, shade, and effect, chiaroscuro, distance, colour, hardness, softness, tint, and so on through the critic's vocabulary.

How differently Ruskin went to work! He studied hard: learned to paint under J. D. Harding and Copley Fielding, and then, when he was familiar with the methods by which effects are produced—in a word, an artist himself—he wrote about art.

How carefully he laboured to acquire knowledge in his favourite pursuit may be illustrated by this simple confession. 'The winter,' he says, 'was spent mainly in trying to get at the mind of Titian—not a light winter's task; of which the issue, being in many ways very unexpected to me, necessitated my going in the spring to Berlin to see Titian's portrait of Lavinia there, and to Dresden to see "The Tribute Money," the elder Lavinia, and Girl in White with the flag fan. Another portrait at Dresden of a lady in a dress of rose and gold—by me unheard of before—and one of an admiral at Munich, had like to have kept me in Germany all the summer.'

How different such work as this from that of the critic who learnt harmony and thorough bass in three lessons, and then thought fit to

> Assume the god—
> Affect to nod

on the merits of every new composition! But those times have probably gone by for ever, as far as the better class of London journals is concerned, though the artistic and literary criticism of country papers is at this day funny in the extreme.

We have said that the first volume of Ruskin's great work met with an indifferent reception at the hands of the literary critics of the year 1843. But the book made its way—indeed, it was impossible that it should be otherwise—and its author became famous. One axiom forms the basis of the work: 'The art is greatest which conveys the greatest number of great ideas.' The first volume shows what painters have best imitated Nature. The second treats of Beauty, *typical* and *vital*. Perhaps this volume contains the finest of Ruskin's writing. The subject, almost illimitable, is treated with a master's hand. The author of 'Modern Painters' has produced a book which has no parallel in any European language. It is impossible here to do any justice even to an outline of its contents, and we do not attempt it, but refer our readers to the book itself.

So far, we have spoken chiefly of his magnum opus. Mr. Ruskin's other works are, 'Seven Lamps of Architecture,' 1849; 'The Stones of Venice,' 1851-53; 'Construction of Sheepfolds;' 'Two Paths;' 'Harbours of England;' 'Political Economy of Art;' 'Unto this Last;' 'Sesame and Lilies;' 'Ethics of Dust;' 'Kings' Treasuries and Queens' Gardens;' 'War, Commerce, and Work;' 'Letters to a Working Man;' 'A Wreath of Wild Olives.'

There is no more honoured name in contemporary English literature than that of John Ruskin. In his books he has discharged the noblest functions of a writer; but it were enough to make him famous in his generation had he done no more than teach our Philistine art-critics what is the true standard to which art criticism should be raised.

W. H. SMITH, M.P.

PORTRAITS of the Member for Westminster have been published in various illustrated papers since he was successful in carrying off the 'blue ribbon' among electioneering contests in November 1868; and his features are now as well known to the public as those of any member of the House of Commons not a minister, ex-minister, or great party leader.

Mr. Smith was born in London in 1825, and is the head of the firm of W. H. Smith & Son, 186 Strand, whose various branch establishments, in the shape of railway book-stalls, are familiar to every traveller. The great house in the Strand was founded by the father of the subject of the present memoir. Forty years ago, when the London daily papers were fresh in the north of England forty-eight hours after their publication in the metropolis, when London and Manchester were that distance of time apart, all newspapers sent into the country passed through the Post Office. It occurred to Mr. Smith that, instead of waiting for the night mail and the agency of the Post Office, the morning papers might be sent off by the early morning coaches. As the earliest editions of the papers were often later than the times fixed for the departure of the coaches, Mr. Smith had great trouble to catch them. To overcome this difficulty, he established a system of express carts, which rattled along the turnpikes after the morning coaches till they caught them. On occasions of the greatest importance, these expresses of Mr. Smith's went the whole way—at a great expense, of course. For instance, Smith's express messenger, with newspapers conveying the news of George IV.'s death, arrived in Dublin before the king's messenger reached that city.

Coaches went out and railways came in. Mr. Smith, first in the coaching days, was first under the new régime, and from the beginning has supplied almost every traveller by railway with his newspaper and his book. The enterprise and successes of the house, culminating in the election of

COMMON SENSE.

the head of the firm to fill the place of John Stuart Mill, as representative of one of the first constituencies in the kingdom, would afford matter for a fine chapter in commercial history.

Mr. William Henry Smith is a liberal Conservative in politics, an active member of the London School Board, a magistrate for the county of Herts, and a member of the Council of King's College. An able and ready debater, in the House of Commons his speeches are always listened to with marked attention, and his opinions carry great weight with them. The Member for Westminster addresses the House only when he has something of real importance to say. He is active in the discharge of his parliamentary duties, an invaluable man on committees, and has as high a reputation as any member of the House for the possession of that too rare quality—sound common sense.

THOMAS CARLYLE.

Thomas Carlyle, the 'Philosopher of Chelsea,' and one of the most prominent and original writers of his time, was born almost in the last lustrum of the last century. At Ecclefechan, in Dumfriesshire, he first saw the light, on the 4th of December 1795. All we can attempt will be to jot down some of the more noteworthy incidents in his life. To try to criticise the writings, to make a correct estimate of the genius of Carlyle, and endeavour to indicate his future place among the writers of his age, would take a volume, if the work were fairly done. Most writers who have had him under notice have said this, and in their next paragraph have fallen into vulgar abuse or more vulgar panegyric. Another trick we have seen nearly every writer of an essay on Carlyle fall into is imitation of his uncouth style and unwarrantable words. Some of the reviewers have gone farther than this: they have tried an imitation of his ideas. This last effort has been a signal failure. He is original. But every reader of his works who has the slightest respect for the language which was sufficient for the needs of a Milton, a Shakespeare, or a Burke, will heartily regret that the Chelsea philosopher ever went to live in Germany, or, at least, that he ever departed from the simple and flowing style of his earliest works; as, for instance, 'The Life of Schiller,' published in 1824. However, it is too late now for criticisms on his style to be of any use. His works are written; and, as they are full of great thoughts, the ugliness of their diction will always be forgotten in the originality, truth, and power of their matter.

Thomas Carlyle is the son of a Scotch farmer, by whom he was educated as thoroughly as possible. From the parish school at Ecclefechan he went to a school at Annan, and thence, when he was fourteen years old, to the University of Edinburgh. Like most sons of Scotch farmers who have had a good education, Carlyle's first notion was to be made a 'meenester.' But he gave up the ministry for a mathematical tutorship in a school.

A LATTER-DAY PHILOSOPHER.

This most disagreeable drudgery to a man of his genius he quitted in two years to become a professional writer. In this capacity he furnished sixteen articles for Brewster's 'Edinburgh Encyclopædia.' Perhaps the highest praise that can be given to encyclopædia articles written half a century ago is to say that they are worth reading now. He also translated at this time 'Legendre's Geometry,' to which he added a preface on Proportion. In 1824 his German studies bore fruit. 'Wilhelm Meister,' in English, from his pen, appeared in that year.

In 1826 he married, and removed from Edinburgh shortly after to a small estate at Craigenputtock, Dumfriesshire. Here he led a life of seclusion, devoted to study, and writing for the 'Edinburgh,' the 'Westminster,' the 'Foreign Quarterly,' and 'Fraser's.' He lived at Craigenputtock eight years, and then removed, in 1834, to Cheyne-walk, Chelsea, which has been his home for thirty-eight years.

In 1837 he began to give lectures in public. These lectures were continued for several years, and the subjects dealt with were German literature, literary history, 'Revolutions of Modern Europe,' and, in 1840, 'Heroes and Hero Worship.' As a lecturer, our philosopher was remarkable for rough vigour, masterlike handling of his subject, and rude language to his audiences. The last, no doubt, did them good, and did not displease them. They paid to hear and see a nineteenth-century Diogenes, and they got their money's worth, and something more.

Carlyle was made Lord Rector of the University of Edinburgh in 1866, and his speech to the young men of his Alma Mater was one of the finest ever spoken from the Lord Rector's chair. It was in this year that his wife died. This sad event was a great shock. They had been married for forty years; and the epitaph her husband placed on her tombstone is one of the most eloquent and loving memorials ever penned. He came out in August of the same year to defend Governor Eyre from the attacks of his enemies. But his last public appearance of importance was as the writer of the article, 'Shooting Niagara: and After?' which was published in 'Macmillan' just after the passing of the Reform Bill.

J. B. BUCKSTONE.

LIKE many men who, as actors, hold a high place in the estimation of the public, Mr. John Baldwin Buckstone left the profession to which he was brought up to become an actor. He was born in a southern suburb of London, in the year 1802, and was originally in the navy; but gave up the chance of serving his country afloat to become an articled clerk in an attorney's office. The law, however, was not a congenial pursuit; and Mr. Buckstone, having a very strong taste for the drama, made his first appearance on any stage at the Theatre Royal Oakingham, in 1823. At this time he appears to have had a notion of succeeding Garrick as Hamlet, Othello, and Macbeth; but one day, the low comedian being absent, at half an hour's notice he undertook the character of Gabriel, the drunken servant in 'The Children in the Wood.' His success was so marked that he was afterwards induced to pay great attention to such characters. He continued, however, to appear in tragic parts; and for the remainder of the season he played in tragedy and comedy alternately.

Mr. Buckstone's début in London was made in the same year (1823) at the Surrey Theatre, where he played the part of Peter Smink in Payne's 'Armistice.' The success of the performance and the applause that greeted it clearly foreshadowed the position he would occupy on the London boards in low-comedy characters.

His fame reached the Adelphi, and he was offered an engagement there, which he accepted—appearing as Bobby Trot in his own drama of 'Luke the Labourer,' T. P. Cooke playing the Sailor, and Terry the Labourer.

Mr. Buckstone's connection with the Adelphi lasted for many years. He used to play there in the winter, and at the Haymarket in the summer. He is the author of a large number of dramas, most of which were very successful at the time they were produced.

But it is as the lessee of the Haymarket that Mr. Buckstone is best

OF INFINITE JEST.

known to the present generation of playgoers. Mr. Webster took this theatre in 1837, and Mr. Buckstone went there with him, and, we believe, played there until he became lessee himself. As all our readers know, he is to be found there still, where every lover of good acting and a good laugh hopes he will long remain. Among his best impersonations, Box in 'Box and Cox,' Touchstone, Marplot, and Tony Lumpkin may be mentioned; and his most successful dramas are the famous 'Green Bushes,' 'Flowers of the Forest,' and 'The Rough Diamond.' How often his fun and rich drollery have set the house in a roar every playgoer knows. His impersonations are marked by originality of conception; but his strong personality always shines through all, to the delight of all his admirers. On the whole, the modern stage has every reason to be proud of Mr. Buckstone.

FREDERICK LOCKER.

POETS of society are, perhaps, rarer than poets of any other sort. The subject of our cartoon, however, has earned a place in the estimation of lovers of poetry by the side of Praed, and a little in advance of Prior, not only in time, but in skill and taste. Mr. Locker was born in 1821. He is of an old Kentish family: his father, Edward Hawke Locker, was a Civil Commissioner of Greenwich Hospital, a warm patron of literature and art, and the founder of the naval gallery of Greenwich Hospital; he also published the lives of some of the most distinguished naval worthies, as well as a tour that he made in Spain with Earl Russell—his own sketches illustrating the volume. The grandfather of the poet was Captain W. Locker, R.N., under whom both Lord Nelson and Lord Collingwood served. The former was especially his old and attached friend. In one of the numerous letters from Lord Nelson to his grandfather, in the possession of Mr. Locker, Lord Nelson says: 'You were the first person to teach me how to board a Frenchman, by your conduct when in the Experiment. You said, "Lay a Frenchman close, and you will beat him."' Captain Locker died Lieutenant-Governor of Greenwich Hospital.

Mr. Frederick Locker married a sister of the late Earl of Elgin and Kincardine, by whom he has one daughter.

Mr. Locker has at different times contributed original verse to the 'Times,' 'Pall-Mall Gazette,' 'Blackwood,' 'Cornhill,' 'Once a Week,' 'Punch,' the 'Owl,' 'Macmillan,' 'Good Words,' 'St. Pauls,' and other magazines. Writing to a friend, his experience makes him say: 'Do not despair. At first I had great difficulty in persuading editors to have anything to say to my verses. They were unanimous in declining them; but

A MELANCHOLY JESTER.

'I only wear the cap and bells,
And yet some tears are in my verses.'

Thackeray believed in me, and used to say, "Never mind, Locker; our verse *may* be small beer, but at any rate it is the right tap." This encouraged me, and I wrote on; and when "Macmillan" refused "My Neighbour Rose," I sent it to "The Cornhill;" and when "Fraser" declined "A Nice Correspondent," I sent it to "St. Pauls." I could get no one to accept "My Grandmother." What used particularly to discourage me was, having my verses returned as not suitable, and then to see in the very next number of the magazine a poem that gave me the impression that it was the work of some relative of the editor—perhaps his grandmamma. I think, if I wrote now, the editors would be more amiable; but it is too late, and this is what may be called the irony of destiny.'

This may be so: it may be hard for a poet to find he has grown tired of writing just at the time when his verses are welcome everywhere; but the author of the exquisite little volume of 'London Lyrics' may safely rest on his laurels. Thackeray, seldom at fault in his literary criticisms, was quite right in this instance. The verses are anything but small beer. They are gems of the utmost polish and beauty. That they are appreciated, a fifth edition is of itself sufficient evidence. A writer in the 'Contemporary Review' for July, in an article on the genius of Prior, Praed, and Locker, makes the following remarks, which we should be wrong if we refrained from quoting. Let us premise that in 1867 Messrs. Moxon published a volume, edited by Mr. Locker, called 'Lyra Elegantiarum,' which was a collection of the best English vers de société. To this volume the editor contributed a charmingly written introduction, in which he set out at length the various qualifications indispensable to any poet's production of unimpeachable vers de société. Upon this preface the 'Contemporary' reviewer comments thus :

'Among the qualifications of a poet of society, the following may be insisted on as indispensable. He must before all things be a man of the world, educated up to a high level of contemporary culture, and gifted with that temper of mental health which, as Goethe says, can only be obtained by him who "lives in the universal way with multitudes of men." He must be privileged, either by right of birth or force of wit, to move in the "upper" circle of the social sphere, and will be the fitter for his office as its prophet, the more he is acquainted with the circles below it. That he must have a definite artistic bias, a "singing" faculty, or, as Mr. Locker phrases it, must "be more or less of a poet"—cela va sans dire. His next essential qualification is the gift of humour. No society can ever have existed in which youth and beauty, genius and experience, freely commingled, without the atmospheric element of humour, the incessant play of mental summer lightning, produced by the gentle collision of electrical natures. A flow of light humorous talk, rippling with banter, bubbling into jets of wit and satire, is notoriously the staple of "polite" conversation, and the brightest talkers are the most favoured guests. Lastly, and mainly for the same reason, he must be somewhat of an egotist; not only as any poet, if ever so little subjective, must be in becoming the self-conscious type of a class or race, but because the essence of polite conversation which he has to transfigure into art is never perfect unless the individuality of each participant be discernible in the amalgamated flavour of the whole.'

That Mr. Locker not only possesses all the essential qualifications indispensable in a poet of society of the first rank—whether we take his own estimate of what may be necessary or that of his reviewer—every cultivated reader knows. But widely as his 'London Lyrics' have been read, his poetry is no more likely to please as large a circle as the productions of Cowper, Pope, or Tennyson, than the verses of Prior or Praed are likely to do so.

We have spoken of Mr. Locker's verses as reflecting polish and culture in the highest degree; and, apropos of this, it is curious to note that he was almost as old a man when he began to write as Praed was when he left off writing. Though he is essentially the poet of the 'upper ten thousand,' to quote a hackneyed epithet, Mr. Locker's variety in his studies of life recommends him to all tastes.

Here is a poet, unrivalled in his particular line, who has only published verses that fill a couple of hundred pages. Would that all those other poets —true and sham—would follow his example! Yet by how few lines will any one of them be remembered by an ungrateful posterity! Tennyson said, some time since, to a friend: 'If I am remembered a hundred years hence by twenty lines I have written, I shall be a lucky man.' Mr. Locker has written twenty poems that will be remembered a hundred years hence;

as long as style in verse-making is an object of study. Of their kind, his verses are perfect. Having said this, it is unnecessary to praise his ear for rhythm, his skill in rhyme, his taste, his culture, his observation, or the genius that moves to all.

MARK TWAIN.

The name by which the American humorist who wrote 'The Jumping Frog' is known by the readers of his works is a nom de plume. Mr. Samuel L. Clemens has only lately left England, and has promised to come and see us 'Britishers' again before long.

California has developed a literature of its own, and its proudest boast is the possession of Mark Twain. 'The Jumping Frog,' pronounced by the 'Saturday Review' 'an inimitably funny book,' soon made its author famous, and gained for him readers wherever English is spoken. 'The Jumping Frog' is a story of the Californian gold-mines; it is very humorous and very well told. 'Eye-openers,' 'Screamers,' 'A Burlesque Autobiography,' 'The Innocents Abroad,' and 'The New Pilgrim's Progress,' are all of them works of the peculiar humour invented by our American cousins, from the pen of the author of 'The Jumping Frog.'

In the summer of the year '67 a pleasure trip left New York, Mark Twain being one of the excursionists. For 1250 dollars, passengers were to cross the Atlantic, and visit Spain, Italy, Turkey, Greece, Egypt, and Syria. The incidents of travel and impressions of life in foreign parts are detailed by the American humorist in the two last works of the list given above. 'The Innocents Abroad' gives Twain's account of the voyage out; while 'The New Pilgrim's Progress' recounts the adventures of the voyage home.

The author of these books is possessed of remarkable talent. His works are widely read and very generally popular. Mark Twain is altogether the best living exponent of American humour, and he may be sure of receiving a hearty welcome whenever he revisits the Old Country.

AMERICAN HUMOUR.

H. M. STANLEY.

RATHER more than three years ago—on the 16th of October 1869—Mr. Henry M. Stanley, travelling correspondent of the 'New York Herald,' being then in Madrid, received a telegram from the proprietor of that journal calling him to Paris. The message from Mr. James Gordon Bennett was to this effect: 'Come to Paris on important business.'

The nature of this business was communicated to Mr. Stanley in the following conversation, quoted from the introductory chapter of his book:

Mr. Bennett asked:
'Where do you think Livingstone is?'
'I really do not know, sir.'
'Do you think he is alive?'
'He may be, and he may not be,' I answered.
'Well, I think he is alive, and that he can be found; and I am going to send you to find him.'
Mr. Bennett goes on to say:
'Of course you will act according to your own plans, and do what you think best. BUT FIND LIVINGSTONE.'

More easily said than done. But to the great honour of the young correspondent of the New York paper, it will ever be set down, in the pages of the history of gallant adventure, that he successfully accomplished the difficult task of finding Dr. Livingstone in Central Africa. This came to pass two years after Mr. Stanley received his instructions from Mr. Bennett. On Friday the 10th of November 1871, at the village of Ujiji, the young explorer shook the famous missionary by the hand. When he saw Livingstone advancing to meet him, he was overpowered with joy at the welcome sight of the object of his long search. 'What would I not have given,' he says, 'for a bit of friendly wilderness where, unseen, I might vent my joy

HE FOUND LIVINGSTONE.

in some mad freak, such as idiotically biting my hand, turning a somersault, or slashing at trees, in order to allay those exciting feelings that were well-nigh uncontrollable. My heart beats fast; but I must not let my face betray my emotions, lest it should detract from the dignity of a white man appearing under such extraordinary circumstances.'

The circumstances of such a meeting as that of the two travellers are indeed unique. It is not to be wondered at that Mr. Stanley wanted to 'kick up his heels' on the occasion.

Reviews of his book, 'How I found Livingstone,' reports of his receptions and speeches, and of dinners given in his honour, have filled the columns of the daily and weekly press to such an extent as to render a review of Mr. Stanley's travels in extenso unnecessary. We may, however, remark that, as a narrator of the incidents of travel and adventure, he is far behind several of his predecessors in 'doing Africa.' Grant, Speke, Du Chaillu, and Burton have all written more picturesque accounts of their performances. Mr. Stanley's book only becomes interesting when the reader is more than half way through its pages. From the time he records his meeting with Livingstone, however, the interest in his doings becomes supreme.

There are two gentlemen who have travelled who could have done justice to the subject. Mr. Sala and Mr. Hepworth Dixon could both have given us a series of picturesque sketches of such an adventure, unrivalled in their way. There was, however, the little difficulty of getting to Ujiji. This it was, probably, that deterred them both from writing a book of travels that would have put all their previous performances into the shade. There remains the fact that Mr. Stanley did get there. This places his book beyond the pale of ordinary criticism. His readers will never forget that he found Livingstone. In the knowledge of this, any literary faults he may have will be readily pardoned.

J. A. FROUDE.

Our ablest historians devote their learning and energies nowadays rather to giving a complete history of a comparatively short period than to recording the history of a country from what are known as 'the earliest times' down to 'the present day.' Prominent among these writers of history is Mr. Froude. An original thinker, a sound scholar, and a man of varied culture and of large and liberal ideas, his opinions are always worthy of attention, though it is not at all times easy to draw the same conclusions that he does from statements of historical facts. Mr. Froude's principal works are 'Short Studies on Great Subjects,' a 'History of England from the Fall of Wolsey to the Defeat of the Spanish Armada,' 'The Nemesis of Faith,' 'The English in Ireland,' vol. i. This work is to be completed in two volumes. Under the title of 'Short Studies on Great Subjects,' Mr. Froude has collected several of his essays—historical, controversial, and descriptive—originally published in 'Fraser's Magazine' and elsewhere. Mr. Froude's literary style is very attractive. The diction is always simple and pure, but there is an animation and spirit in the historian's descriptions sufficient to clothe with interest the barest facts, figures, and arguments of his historical narratives.

James Anthony Froude was born on the 23d of April 1818. He took deacon's orders in the Church of England in 1844; published 'The Nemesis of Faith' in 1849, the 'History' from 1856 to 1869, the 'Short Studies' in 1867, 'English in Ireland' in 1872.

HISTORY.

SHIRLEY BROOKS.

The editorship of 'Punch' necessarily confers upon its holder a prominent position among men of letters; but the present occupant of the editorial chair was an eminent man of letters, as well as a tried and valued collaborateur on the staff of the comic paper, before he filled the difficult position of its literary chief. When Mark Lemon died in 1870, a few weeks before his friend Charles Dickens was taken from us, everybody felt, as was said of Garrick, and also of Lever, that his loss was the removal of a light the extinction of which eclipsed the gaiety of nations. It is often unknown to the world by whom a popular paper is edited, but Mark Lemon's name was familiar in their mouths as a household word—to quote the now hackneyed line of the poet, of whose Falstaff the first editor of 'Punch' was so excellent a representative. The name of Mark Lemon was known all over the English-speaking world, and everywhere 'Punch' connoted Lemon. The two ideas were inseparable from the term. But when the first grief at the loss of the genial and witty humorist had had time to lose some of its poignancy, all who wished well to the satirical journal—in other words, all the world—were rejoiced to hear that the choice of his successor had fallen on Shirley Brooks: like the original projector of 'Punch,' himself a novelist, humorist, playwright, and—to employ a phrase in use in the cricket-field—'good all-round' man of letters.

The promise implied in his selection has been well borne out, and 'Punch' has rarely —take it one month with another—been more amusing and clever, or more brightly lighted with honest yet kindly satire, than it has been since Shirley Brooks has driven the team of artists and men of letters that make up the staff of the English 'Charivari.'

The subject of our notice was born in 1815, and after his education—as far as youthful studies are concerned—was completed, he turned his

PUNCH.

attention to the law, and passed with great success the examinations of the Incorporated Law Society. But, like Dickens and Disraeli, the natural bent of his genius impelled him towards the culture of the Muses, and he forsook law for literature.

He was for some years associated with the 'Morning Chronicle;' and, as the representative of that paper, travelled over Russia, Syria, and Egypt, being charged with an inquiry into the state of the labouring classes in those countries.

As a dramatist, the editor of 'Punch' has produced works of sterling merit. 'The Creole, or Love's Fetter,' was first produced at the Lyceum in April 1847, in which Mr. and Mrs. Keeley, Frank Matthews, and Leigh Murray sustained the principal characters. The next year saw, at the same theatre, a capital one-act comedy, 'Anything for a Change,' in which Harley and Charles Mathews appeared. Among his other dramatic works, we may mention 'The Daughter of the Stars,' brought out at the Strand. In 'Timour the Tartar' he had John Oxenford as joint author. 'The Guardian Angel,' at the Haymarket, Mr. and Mrs. Keeley appeared in; and 'The Lowther Arcade,' a very sprightly farce, with two pieces of greater labour, 'Honours and Tricks,' and 'Our New Governess,' must not be omitted from this list.

Mr. Brooks was in his earlier days a contributor to many of the best periodicals; was a leader writer on the 'Illustrated London News,' and for some time editor of the 'Literary Gazette;' but it is as a novelist that his talents are best known and appreciated by the readers of 'Once a Week,' in which his best stories have appeared; and were it not that we propose to let him tell us the history of that famous satirical journal he now so worthily conducts, we should dwell at length on his novels. 'The Silver Cord,' which appeared in 'Once a Week,' 'Sooner or Later,' 'The Gordian Knot,' and his first story, 'Aspen Court,' complete the list of his longer works of fiction. Nothing would be more to our mind than to offer some criticism here upon the skill in the construction of plots, the sustained interest, the sparkling dialogue, and the touches of genius in exhibiting the inner working of the human heart, that his novels show; but instead we will give, in Mr. Shirley Brook's own words, the story of how 'Punch' was founded, and how it became the most successful of satirical and comic journals.

'Punch,' said its present editor, in a very charming and witty lecture he used to deliver on 'Modern Satire,' 'was founded July 17th, 1841, by two or three gentlemen—Henry Mayhew, the original projector, Mark Lemon, E. Landells, Sterling Coyne, and Henry Grattan. It was at first a joint speculation of authors, artists, and engravers; and I was only connected with it after it had been established, and others had borne the heat and burden of the day. The first and second numbers were brought out; but, in truth, it was a question whether the third would appear, for want of funds, for it was no secret that the projectors were none of them rich men. Indeed, I may say they were all poor men. Had it not been for the happy accident of Mr. Mark Lemon having a farce, "The Silver Thimble," accepted at one of the minor theatres, "Punch" would have been stopped. The silver thimble, however, was large enough to cover the acorn, which has since grown into an oak. At first, the paper was published by a person who was noted as being connected with some disreputable prints, and there was an ill-odour resulting from the connection hanging about "Punch." This was no fault of the projectors; and the moment they were aware of the fact, they took the paper to a respectable firm, who became the proprietors; and from that time the paper has increased largely from year to year in popularity and circulation. Perhaps a good reason why "Punch" has been successful lies in the fact that there has been no line, from the first to the last, which might not be read by a girl of eighteen. Had it been otherwise, I hope I should not have been in this hall to talk about it.'

Speaking of the old contributors, the lecturer referred to Douglas Jerrold (born in London in 1803, died 8th of June 1857), whose writings under the signature of Q., the first of which appeared on the 13th September 1841, were very successful, and soon gained notoriety. The late Gilbert à'Beckett (born in London, 1810; died at Boulogne, 1856) was another valued contributor. The sketch of a London magistrate in 'Aspen Court' is a portrait of Mr. à'Beckett by the hand of his friend, Shirley Brooks. John Leech, who was born in London in 1816, was mentioned in appropriate terms of eulogy. 'The greatest compliment that could be paid to him was that of some young ladies who were too far from a town to procure the fashions early, so they dressed themselves after the style of his caricatures.' Albert Smith (1816-1860) was an able contributor. Thomas Hood (1778-1845), whose various pen touched alike the springs of laughter and the sources of tears, was amongst those who wrote for 'Punch.' This is the story of the publication of the celebrated 'Song of the Shirt.' Hood sent it to Mark Lemon, for insertion in 'Punch,' with a note of apology. 'I sent it to a first-rate magazine, and they wrote back, "It is hardly the thing for genteel people."' 'What say you?' said Shirley Brooks. The answer of his audience need hardly be told—how their applause recorded their appreciation of the writings of Thomas Hood.

Tom Taylor, born at Sunderland in 1817, was also a contributor. Perceval Leigh—whose name was not so well known, but 'Pips his Diary,' and 'Ye Manners and Customs of ye English in ye Nineteenth Century,' &c., were from his pen—Henry and Horace Mayhew, Laman Blanchard, Maguire, Thackeray, Tennyson, Trench, were also among the writers; and Doyle, who drew the design for the cover—which, by the bye, is not the original one in which Mr. 'Punch' first showed—and Kenny Meadows were among the illustrators. The names of those of the present time are too well known to need mention here.

Shirley Brooks said, 'The cartoons were settled at a dinner given once a week, at which the editor met the contributors and artists. These meetings were most pleasant, and the dinners remarkably good.'

He farther related some humorous anecdotes of the curious communications forwarded to the editor. 'Ladies sometimes sent accounts of the dresses, ribbons, and bonnets of other persons, with a request to "cut them up," the information being of so minute a character that it could only be written by one lady of another. Sometimes the editor was requested to write something stinging about persons who gave parties and did not pay their debts, laying special stress on those who crammed 120 guests into a room not capable of holding fifty.

'Some persons were patronising; and one gentleman sought to bribe, by stating he, if something he sent were inserted, would take twenty copies of "Punch." Sometimes artful advertisers sent communications deprecatory of themselves, hoping to get notoriety; but Mark Lemon was too old to be sold in that way'—as no doubt Shirley Brooks is.

'An hotel-keeper,' he added, 'who had lately opened a house in a watering-place, pleasantly situated, offered, if a cut of his premises were inserted, and a couple of letters were written and dated from his house, in the pages of "Punch," to let any two gentlemen connected with the office stay at his hotel free of charge for a month.' On one occasion, when the lecturer was in a railway carriage, the talk turned on 'Punch,' and a fellow passenger informed him in confidence that he had written a series of papers in the periodical of which Shirley Brooks himself was the author.

Our outline of the remarks the lecturer made on the history of 'Punch' is necessarily very imperfect. But the lecture on 'Satire' was altogether a very charming evening's entertainment. We wish the editor of 'Punch' would repeat it. We close this notice by quoting a few words from James Hannay's estimate of the satire of 'Punch:' 'The decorum which distinguishes "Punch" from the best effusions of the class in the olden days belongs as much to the age as to the periodical. In the worst of times our facetious friend is innocent; and though our progenitors seem to have thought that all wit required great license, the student finds that they were often licentious and dull too, sacrificing decency, and getting nothing in exchange.'

Shirley Brooks, in accepting the duty of carrying out the traditional policy of the leading satirical journal on all social and political questions, in taking the chair so long and so well filled by one of the first promoters of the paper, and in essaying to maintain the prestige of the best journal of the kind in the world, took upon himself a grave responsibility. For 'Punch' belongs to the British nation. This step was taken two years ago. The result has proved how happy was the selection of a successor to him who had grown old with the paper, whose interests he watched so well— how capable and how gentle a follower has been found to hold the coachman's whip over the flyers that pull the 'Punch' coach.

> Cursed be verse, how well soe'er it flow,
> That tends to make one honest man my foe.

Ten years ago, this couplet closed the lecturer's comments on the paper he now edits. The thoroughly English sentiment that inspires this homely rhyme is the yeast that leavens the fancy, wit, and satire which so often have lighted the pages of our Fleet-street friend. The name of Shirley Brooks is a guarantee of the maintenance of the old principles in the 'Punch' of the future.

DEAN STANLEY.

The Very Reverend Arthur Penrhyn Stanley is the son of a clergyman who was at one time in the navy, and who, though he was made Bishop of Norwich, was always a good deal more remarkable for his knowledge of natural history than for his theological learning.

He was educated at Rugby School, under Arnold, afterwards proceeding to Balliol, where he won a scholarship. The Broad-Church leader's University course was distinguished by a series of successes, ending, in 1837, in his taking a First Class in Classics. He was elected to a fellowship at University; and for many years, and with signal success and popularity, Dean Stanley discharged the duties of tutor of his college.

He was afterwards Regius Professor of Ecclesiastical History at Oxford, and Canon of Christ Church.

Nearly thirty years ago, Dean Stanley first became known to the world of letters outside the limits of his University by the publication, in 1844, of his admirably written 'Life of Arnold.'

He is also the author of many volumes of sermons and lectures, and has contributed largely to periodical literature.

He travelled in the East with the Prince of Wales, and was, no doubt, a most suitable chaplain, and appreciated by his Royal Highness at his true worth. When in the East, Dr. Stanley let his beard grow long, which gave him a patriarchal appearance he does not wear in London, where many are familiar with the figure of the small, thin, spiritual-looking man who is Dean of Westminster. Dr. Stanley's views in Church matters are well known. He is a leader of the Broad-Church party, is always for the fullest amount of religious liberty for everybody, is a friend of Dr. Colenso's, and was a subscriber to the Voysey Defence Fund.

Dr. Stanley succeeded the present Archbishop Trench in the Deanery of Westminster. His official position at the abbey church has placed

BROAD CHURCH.

upon him the duty of preaching a funeral sermon over the mortal remains of several very great men. Dean Stanley has preached, after their burial in the national mausoleum, the funeral sermons of Charles Dickens, Grote, and other eminent men. Such a painful task could not have fallen into abler or more friendly hands.

The Dean's prominent figure among the ecclesiastical reformers has subjected him to much severe criticism. In that pretty Church speech at Oxford, in the month of November 1864, when Mr. Disraeli told the world that he espoused the side of the angels, he alluded thus to the labours of Stanley, Jowett, and Maurice:

'I do perfect justice to the great talent, the great energy, and the considerable information which the new party command; but I believe that this new party in the Church will fail, for two reasons. In the first place, having examined all their writings, I believe without an exception — whether they consist of fascinating eloquence, diversified learning, and picturesque sensibility—I speak seriously what I feel—all these exercised, too, by one honoured in this great University, and whom to know is to admire and regard—or whether I find them in the cruder conclusions of prelates, who appear to me to have commenced their theological studies after they grasped the crozier, and who introduced to society their obsolete discoveries . . . . or whether I read the lucubrations of nebulous professors, who appear in their style to have revived chaos . . . . or, lastly, whether it be the provincial arrogance and precipitate self-complacency which flash and glare in an essay or review—I find this common characteristic of all their writings, that their learning is always second-hand.'

Notwithstanding such criticism, the 'new school' still lives, and very likely now Mr. Disraeli himself would be prepared to treat it with more respect.

MATTHEW ARNOLD.

The great apostle to the Philistines of this later age, and the preacher of sweetness and light, Matthew Arnold, is the eldest son of one of the most remarkable and noblest Englishmen who have flourished in the nineteenth century—Dr. Thomas Arnold, some time head-master of Rugby School.

Matthew Arnold was born December 24th, 1822, at Laleham, near Staines, county Middlesex. He was the eldest son of nine children of his distinguished father, of whom he is as good a representative as the present Lord Derby is of the illustrious Tory chief.

The Arnolds came originally from Lowestoft, in Suffolk, but the grandfather of the poet and critic was a collector of customs dues at Cowes, in the Isle of Wight.

Matthew Arnold was educated first at Winchester and Rugby. From school he went to Oxford, where he was entered at Balliol, having gained a scholarship. This was in 1840.

During his university career he gained the Newdigate prize for English verse, the subject of his prize poem being Oliver Cromwell. At the end of his term in statu pupillari he graduated in honours, and was elected a fellow of Oriel; and in 1847 was appointed private secretary to the late Marquis of Lansdowne, which post he held for four years. He married, in 1851, the daughter of the late Mr. Justice Wightmann, and received from Government the appointment of lay inspector of schools, a post he was particularly well qualified to fill with advantage to the cause of education.

The first volume of his poems was published in 1849, as the work of 'A.;' and only a limited circle of friends knew the name of the author of 'The Strayed Reveller,' and other poems. Three years afterwards 'Empedocles on Etna' appeared, and shortly after that the 'A.' was dropped, and Messrs. Longmans issued a volume of poems, the authorship of which was avowed.

SWEETNESS AND LIGHT.

Matthew Arnold's poems are full of original thoughts, expressed in the purest English. They are models of style; but, from their subject-matter and treatment, are never likely to be popular, in a wide sense of the word. To these published books of verse he owed his selection for the post of Professor of Poetry in the University of Oxford; an important office he held for ten years, from 1857 to 1867. His most remarkable lectures in this time are on the subject of translating Homer, in which he advocates, in very strong language, the adoption of the English hexameter, in preference to any other metre, for effectively rendering the great Greek poet in English verses.

Mr. Arnold is chiefly remarkable in prose as an essayist. Perhaps his best-known book is that entitled 'Essays on Criticism,' which consists of a collection of papers previously published in various magazines and reviews.

HARRISON AINSWORTH.

Mr. William Harrison Ainsworth, whose novels were very popular only few years ago, and who is still a contributor to Mr. Mudie's bookshelves, was born at Manchester, in the year 1805. He was educated at the Free Grammar School of his native city, and, the son of a solicitor, was bred to the law. But at a very early age Mr. Ainsworth showed a taste for literature; before he left school he was a contributor to the pages of 'The Iris,' a journal then published in Manchester. He married the daughter of Mr. Ebers, a publisher in Bond-street, and at that time manager of the Opera-house. Ainsworth's first novel was 'Sir John Chiverton;' and of this, his first essay in fiction, no less an authority than Sir Walter Scott spoke in terms of high praise.

At Mr. Ebers's suggestion, Ainsworth appears to have tried his hand as a publisher; but he soon abandoned this, and devoted himself to literary pursuits. In 1834, 'Rookwood' appeared, and at once established his reputation as a writer of fiction. 'Rookwood' was followed, in 1837, by 'Crichton,' which was as successful as its immediate predecessor, and added to the author's fame. In the month of March 1839, Charles Dickens retired from the editorship of 'Bentley's Miscellany,' and wrote his successor in, in his humorous style, talking of the old and new coachman—'Bentley's' being the coach. 'The new whip'—we quote the writer of a short biography of Ainsworth—'having mounted the box, drove straight to Newgate.' By the bye, Dickens had driven 'Bentley's' there before him; but the great humorist's thieves' story had a fine moral to it. 'He there took in Jack Sheppard and Cruikshank the artist; and, aided by that very vulgar but wonderful draughtsman, he made an efficient story of the burglar's or housebreaker's life.'

In such works of fiction as 'Jack Sheppard,' it soon became plain that Ainsworth's forte lay. He followed up his latest success with 'Guy Fawkes'

THE BIOGRAPHER OF JACK SHEPPARD.

and 'The Tower of London.' In 1842 his connection with 'Bentley's' terminated, and in a magazine of his own he produced successively 'The Miser's Daughter,' 'Windsor Castle,' and 'St. James's.' In the above list the best of the author's novels are contained, but it by no means exhausts the catalogue of his works. It is as the biographer of such gentlemen as Mr. Jack Sheppard, of bad fame, that our author must lay claim to immortality; and it is in this field of labour that he is most at home. He has himself placed on record the state of his feelings after he had disposed of Mr. Turpin's apocryphal steed 'Black Bess.' 'Well do I remember,' says the author, 'the fever into which I was thrown during the time of composition. My pen literally scoured over the pages. So thoroughly did I identify myself with the flying highwayman that, once started, I found it impossible to halt.... In his (Turpin's) company I mounted the hillside, dashed through the bustling village, swept over the desolate heath, threaded the silent street, plunged into the eddying stream.... With him I shouted, sang, laughed, exulted, wept; nor did I retire to rest till in imagination I heard the bell of York Minster toll forth the knell of poor Black Bess.'

This is poetic frenzy with a vengeance; and nobody will be disposed to deny that, whatever else the novelist lacked, it certainly was not sympathy with his creations.

The moral tendency of his writings, and the effect they were likely to produce on the youthful or untrained mind, have often been the subject of criticism. Of these, we think there can be no doubt the effect must be bad. While we wish Mr. Ainsworth no harm, we wish the cause of morality in fiction well; and we cannot help thinking that, if the 'fever into which he was thrown,' by the recital of the lawless adventures of a highwayman, had carried off his passion for writing novels, English literature would have been the gainer.

J. B. HOPKINS.

According to an oft-told story, a parliamentary reporter being asked if a certain M.P. had not been in the gallery, replied, 'Yes; but he was not up to our mark, so we pitched him into the House!' The said M.P. might have been a clever politician and statesman, though he failed in reporting, which requires a special and natural aptitude. The same remark is applicable to other departments of journalism. The leader-writer, the essayist, and the critic need extensive reading, minute observation, quickness of apprehension, and to wield an ever-ready pen. The journalist must also have the faculty of writing in a style that is both easy and instructive; for the newspaper reader expects to be spared the trouble of thinking, and to be regaled with completely digested thought. The adage that tells us the poet is born and the orator made is a rhetorical error; because the poet needs mental culture, and no man can be an orator unless he has the special talent. So with the journalist, who must be both born and made.

Mr. John Baker Hopkins was born in London, on the 10th of April 1830. He is maternally descended from a Staffordshire family, the Bakers, who have been closely allied with the Jennings family, and he is named after his great grandfather, a Wedgbury worthy, whose physical prowess was celebrated in local song.

In April 1862, Mr. Henry Hotze, the commercial agent of the Confederate States, called on Mr. Hopkins, and discussed the expediency of buying the 'Atlas,' and making it the Confederate organ in Europe. Mr. Hopkins suggested that it would be better to start a new paper as the avowed organ of the Confederacy; and this was agreed to. In ten days after this interview —that is, on the 1st May 1862—the first number of the 'Index' appeared, under the joint editorship and management of Messrs. Hotze and Hopkins. At the 1862 meeting of the Social Science Congress, at the London Guild-

AS MILD A MAN AS EVER SCUTTLED SHIP OR CUT A THROAT.

hall, Mr. Hopkins read an elaborate and remarkable statistical paper on the resources of the South; and this paper he soon afterwards reprinted as an introduction to 'The South Vindicated.'

The connection with the 'Index' involved a great deal of labour outside the immediate business of the paper; for the 'Index' was the bureau for information on Southern affairs. Mr. Hopkins was the London correspondent of the 'New York Daily News,' and he also sent occasional letters to the 'Mobile Register.' At the conclusion of the civil war it was intended to carry on the 'Index;' but President Johnson regarded the continued publication of the paper as a proof that the South had not entirely submitted to the Union, and therefore the 'Index' ceased to appear.

From 1864 until 1868, Mr. Hopkins held the responsible appointment of London correspondent to the Paris 'Correspondence Havas'—a lithographic daily sheet of telegrams and news, circulated by imperial authority, and from which the French press took their information. The 'Correspondence Havas' is the oldest press association in Europe, and from it sprang our 'Reuter agency'—Mr. Julius Reuter having been for many years on the 'Havas' staff before he started his useful and successful agency in England.

In September 1865, Mr. Hopkins was invited by his friend Captain Hamber, the editor, and by Mr. Johnstone, the proprietor, to join the staff of the 'Standard;' and for three years he was associated with that paper.

Meantime Mr. Hopkins produced 'The Fall of the Confederacy,' an essay that was favourably received both in England and America. Some sketches of social life which had been contributed to the 'Cosmopolitan' were collected and published under the title of 'Cosmopolitan Sketches.' A few months after the passing of the 1867 Reform Bill, Mr. Hopkins wrote 'The English Revolution.' In that book, after a survey of the political situation, the author advocates certain changes and reforms which he deems expedient in consequence of the establishment of household suffrage.

At the commencement of 1867, Mr. Hopkins's learned friend, the editor of the 'Law Journal,' offered him an appointment on that paper, which he accepted and still holds. Mr. Hopkins was an occasional contributor of leaders to the 'Morning Post,' and for some time wrote a weekly letter under the signature of 'Esse Quam Videri.'

These letters led to an engagement on 'Vanity Fair,' to which periodical he contributed under the same nom de plume.

In May 1870, the London 'Figaro,' one of the most successful journalistic enterprises of the day, was started; and, two months later, Mr. James Mortimer selected Mr. Hopkins for his chief leader-writer. It cannot be denied that Mr. Hopkins is sometimes too unsparing and too vehement in the use of invective, and too bitter in his satire; but he says, and truly, that he has never written a line that assailed or reflected upon the private character of any man, be he prince or peasant.

GEORGE MACDONALD.

The subject of our cartoon was born in Scotland in the year 1824. He is well known as the editor of 'Good Words for the Young,' the title of which has lately been changed to 'Good Things.' The periodical over the interests of which Mr. Macdonald presides was started after the great success that attended its parent, 'Good Words,' when under the care of the late Dr. Norman Macleod.

Mr. Macdonald's first attempt at a book of any importance was met with a rebuff from the eminent publisher to whom he had offered the manuscript. He received a note, the terms of which are familiar to every man of letters, successful or unsuccessful.

He was told that, though the manuscript was a credit to him, and showed signs of great promise for the future, it contained certain things that it was not desirable, &c. In a word, the copy was politely declined. After this, however, Mr. Macdonald, with the perseverance of his nation, tried again, and was successful.

The book the first eminent publisher had rejected was 'David Elginbrod,' the author's best novel.

The following is a pretty complete list of Mr. Macdonald's works: 'Phantastes,' 'David Elginbrod,' 'The Portent,' 'Alec Forbes of Howglen,' 'Annals of a Quiet Neighbourhood,' 'Guild Court,' 'At the Back of the North Wind,' 'Dealings with the Fairies,' 'Robert Falconer,' 'The Seaboard Parish,' 'Ronald Bannerman's Boyhood,' 'The Miracles of our Lord,' 'Unspoken Sermons,' 'Wilfrid Cumbermede,' and 'The Vicar's Daughter.' Mr. Macdonald's first books displayed considerable originality of thought; the characters were strongly marked and life-like, and they had a good Scotch savour about them. Since then, however, their author has been on the decline; his books have grown dull, and he has taken to favouring his

GOODY GOODY.

readers with long and troublesome sermons in every other chapter of what he is pleased to style new novels.

The fall of the once ubiquitous A. K. H. B.—as far as current literature was concerned—may be traced to foisting upon the public a book of sermons as 'The Graver Thoughts of a Country Parson.' Mr. Macdonald should take warning in time, and call novels novels and sermons sermons.

We should rejoice to see him again writing such books as 'Annals of a Quiet Neighbourhood' and 'David Elginbrod;' and we very much regret he ever devoted himself to goody-goody literature.

WILLIAM TINSLEY.

Among our portraits are included some few of those gentlemen who, not being known in the strict sense as literary men, are identified with literary interests. We have already given Mr. W. H. Smith, M.P. for Westminster, and Mr. Mudie, the well-known librarian; we now add Mr. William Tinsley, of 18 Catherine-street, Strand, the proprietor of 'Tinsleys' Magazine,' whom we have selected as a representative publisher.

Mr. William Tinsley trades under the name of Tinsley Brothers; he has, however, no brother in partnership with him, nor has he had for several years past. The business known as 'Tinsley Brothers' was founded some twenty years ago by William and Edward Tinsley, hence the name under which the business is still carried on by the surviving partner. Mr. Edward Tinsley was, we believe, the younger brother of the two, and at his death, six or seven years ago, the business came into the sole possession of the present proprietor.

William Tinsley was born, in the year 1830, at the village of South Mimms, in the county of Middlesex; and we hope we are violating no confidence when we mention that he was sent to work by his father as a farmer's boy before he was twelve years old; that the only actual schooling he ever received was at the national school at South Mimms, and this for no more than a few months.

At the age of fourteen, young William Tinsley was offered the chance of learning a trade. He availed himself of the opportunity thus afforded him; and it was with the few pounds he had saved whilst working at his trade that he, with his brother Edward, opened a small shop in the Strand for the sale of second-hand books. But the brothers were not long content with being merely booksellers: they soon began to print and publish books on their own account. The few books they published to start with

TINSLEY BROTHERS.

bore the name of William Tinsley only as publisher. Before long they removed to premises in Catherine-street, where the publishing business of the firm of Tinsley Brothers has since that time been carried on.

From a farmer's boy, with two shillings or half a crown a week for wages, to the position Mr. William Tinsley now holds as a publisher, is no ordinary leap in life, especially when it must be taken into consideration that he had only the advantage in early life of the most rudimentary education. Mr. Tinsley is now, we believe, sometimes a contributor upon dramatic and social subjects to the pages of his own magazine. The story of William Tinsley's life, if told at length, would no doubt add but one more to the thousands of proofs of what perseverance and pluck can accomplish when put to the test.

※ The Editor of this volume, and indeed Mr. William Tinsley himself, are both aware that the short statement of the rise and progress of the firm of Tinsley Brothers, and the few particulars about Mr. Tinsley's own life, will be interesting to but a small portion, if any, of the reading public; nor would the statement have been put forth but for very good reasons.

THE END.

LONDON:
ROBSON AND SONS, PRINTERS, PANCRAS ROAD, N.W.

Milton Keynes UK
Ingram Content Group UK Ltd.
UKHW050229030124
435374UK00005B/69